DIVINE FAVORS
GRANTED TO ST. JOSEPH

The Death of Saint Joseph,
"Patron of a Happy Death"

DIVINE FAVORS GRANTED TO ST. JOSEPH

by

Pere Binet, S.J.

Translated by M. C. E. From
The Edition Of The Rev. Fr. Jennesseaux, S.J.

*"Joseph, son of David, fear not to take
unto thee Mary thy wife, for that which is
conceived in her, is of the Holy Ghost.
And she shall bring forth a son: and thou
shalt call his name JESUS. For he shall
save his people from their sins."*
—Matt. 1:20-21

TAN BOOKS AND PUBLISHERS, INC.
Rockford, Illinois 61105

Library of Congress Catalog Card No.: 82-50590

ISBN: 0-89555-187-X

Printed and bound in the United States of America.

TAN BOOKS AND PUBLISHERS, INC.
P.O. Box 424
Rockford, Illinois 61105

1983

CONTENTS

Contents

PRAYER TO ST. JOSEPH, PATRON OF THE UNIVERSAL CHURCH

O MOST powerful patriarch, St. Joseph, patron of that universal Church, which has always invoked thee in anxieties and tribulations; from the lofty seat of thy glory, lovingly regard the Catholic world. Let it move thy paternal heart to see the mystical spouse of Christ and His vicar weakened by sorrow and persecuted by powerful enemies. We beseech thee, by the most bitter suffering thou didst experience on earth, to wipe away in mercy the tears of the revered pontiff, to defend and liberate him, and to intercede with the Giver of peace and charity, that every hostile power being overcome and every error being destroyed, the whole Church may serve the God of all blessings in perfect liberty. Amen.

DIVINE FAVOURS GRANTED TO ST. JOSEPH.

———◇———

CHAPTER I.

WHO IS ST. JOSEPH, AND WHY DOES HE DESERVE SO MUCH HONOUR?

THE Holy Ghost has willed to make the genealogy of the glorious St. Joseph known to us so exactly, that we need only read the Gospels of St. Matthew and St. Luke to be acquainted with all his ancestors. By birth he is a prince of the royal house of David; his ancestors are the patriarchs, the kings of Juda, the great captains of the people of God, the most illustrious among the sons of men. Yet this descendant of David was reduced to obscurity, and lived a poor and humble life.

Divine Favours granted to St. Joseph.

The Evangelists would appear to give Joseph two fathers; but the contradiction is only apparent. St. Luke says he was the son of Heli, who, however, died childless; while St. Matthew calls him the son of Jacob, because, according to several commentators, Jacob, brother of Heli, espoused his sister-in-law Esta as the law of Moses commanded, by whom he had Joseph, who was thus the son of Jacob by nature, and the son of Heli according to the law.

The poverty of the family and the custom of the country obliged Joseph to learn a trade. We do not know positively if he worked in wood or in iron, since the holy Fathers are divided on this point. The more general opinion is, however, that he was a carpenter. St. Justin, in his dialogue with Triphon, adds that the Child Jesus acted as His adopted father's little apprentice, assisting him to make yokes and ploughs.

It is a pious belief of some authors that St. Joseph was sanctified in his mother's womb.*

* Gerson, *Serm. de Nativ. glorios. V.M. et de Commendatione virginei Sponsi ejus Joseph*, Considerat. ii.— Isidor. Isolan., *Summ. de donis S. Joseph*, p. 1, c. ix.

8

Suarez does not go so far. Still we must allow that the partisans of this opinion support it by solid reasons, which have a great appearance of truth.

There can be no doubt that this great Saint was a virgin. Cardinal St. Peter Damian affirms it so positively that he seems to make it an article of faith.* Some learned authors even hold that by a special inspiration of God he made the vow of virginity. Such is the belief of the great chancellor Gerson, of St. Bernardin of Siena, of Suarez, and of several others.†
In any case we cannot doubt that he had lived a pure angelical life when he united himself by chaste bonds to the Virgin Mary, his one and only spouse.

A secret inspiration from heaven caused both Mary and Joseph to contract this alliance, while adoring in their hearts the impenetrable counsel of the great God. Mary was in

* ' Et ne hoc sufficere videatur ut tantummodo virgo sit mater, Ecclesiæ fides est ut virgo fuerit et is, qui simulatus est pater ' (S. Petr. Damian., *Epist.* 1 *ad Nicol. Rom. Pontif.*, c. iii, quæ et opuscul. xvii.).

† Gerson, *Serm. cit.*, Considerat. iii.—Isidor. Isolan., *Summ.*, p. 1, c. xiii.—Suarez, *De Incarnat.*, p. 2, disp. 8, sect 2.—S. Bernardin., *Serm. de S. Joseph*, art. 2, c. i. —S. Thom., p. iii, q. 28, a. 4 ad 3.

her fifteenth year ; the age of Joseph is not known so exactly, tradition being silent on the subject. The opinion that he was about eighty years old is without reasonable grounds, and is not held by theologians, the most esteemed of whom think that he was neither an old man nor a youth, but in the prime of life, between thirty and forty. There are many reasons in support of this opinion, which is now generally held.

Shortly after this virginal marriage had been celebrated with due solemnity, it pleased God to send the Archangel Gabriel to Mary, that he might announce to her the Mystery of the Incarnation, and explain to her that in becoming mother of her Creator, she should not cease to be a virgin: As the mystery was not at once revealed to St. Joseph, he was in sore perplexity, until the Angel of God appearing in a dream, reassured him, by explaining that the fruit of Mary was the work of the Holy Ghost.

The life of the two spouses in this angelic marriage resembled two stars, mutually enlightening each other by their gold and silver rays, without ever coming in contact.

Later, I shall speak of the happiness of this holy life, and with what plenitude of celestial favours God enriched this divine household. For the moment, I shall content myself with showing how the dream of the first Joseph was verified in the second.

The former Joseph saw himself, in a dream, adored by the sun, the moon, and eleven stars. Only later on in Egypt did he understand this vision, when his father, his mother,* and his brethren, prostrate at his feet, adored him as the saviour of the land. The son of the patriarch Jacob was, however, only a type, destined to enhance the splendour of that other Joseph, whom God delighted to make so great, whom Jesus Christ the true Sun of Justice honours as His father, whom Our Lady, called in the Canticles beautiful as the moon, reveres as her lord and spouse, whom the Angels and Saints, who are the stars of heaven, venerate as foster-father and guide of that Infant God, Whose servants they esteem themselves happy to be.

The date of St. Joseph's death is uncertain;

* Not Rachel, who died at the birth of Benjamin, but Bala, Rachel's servant, who was Joseph's nurse, and was like a mother to him (Liran., Tostat. apud Tirin.).

we know only that it took place before the Passion of Our Lord Jesus Christ.* What an entrancing sight to behold him expire, one hand in that of Jesus, the other in that of Our Lady; breathing forth his blessed spirit on the bosom of the Saviour God! To die thus is not to lose life but to overcome death.

Some authors believe, and with reason, that Joseph was among those Saints who, on Ascension Day mounted up to heaven, body and soul, with Jesus Christ. Who indeed deserved more to accompany Jesus in His triumph, than he who accompanied Him so lovingly in His exile in Egypt, and during the laborious pilgrimage of His holy life? We may therefore piously believe that as Jesus, Mary, and Joseph lived united upon earth, bearing the same sufferings, so they now are reunited, body and soul, partaking the same glory. Such is the belief of the devout St. Bernardin of Siena, and even of Suarez, whose usual reserve gives great weight to his

* Gerson, *cit. Serm.*, Considerat. iii.—Isidor. Isolan., *Summ. S. Joseph*, p. 4, c. i.—Suarez, *De Incarnat.*, p. 2, disp. 3, sect. 2.

opinion in this case.* It is true that faith teaches us nothing on this point ; but devotion speaks loudly, and has on its side weighty reasons, and great authorities.

* S. Bernardin., *Serm. de S. Joseph*, art. 3.—Suarez, *De Incarnat.*, p. 2, disp. 8, sect. 2.

CHAPTER II.

IF one may judge of the greatness of the
Saints by the importance of the charges confided to them, St. Joseph must indeed be
marvellously great. St. Peter and St. Paul
in their epistles to the first Christians, claim
only two titles, those of servants and apostles
of Jesus Christ, as being sufficient to prove
the excellence of their vocation. St. John
Chrysostom agrees with them, this double
title being, according to him, more excellent
than that of monarch of the whole earth.*
Now, St. Joseph has many very high titles, and

---

* 'Simon Petrus, servus et apostolus Jesu-Christi'
(2 Pet. i. 1).—'Paulus servus Jesu-Christi, vocatus
apostolus' (Rom. i. 1).—'Dignitatis maximæ loco ponit
illud : Servus Jesu-Christi' (S. Joan. Chrysost. in hunc
locum).

held glorious offices for which he received from God special graces. At present I shall only allude shortly to some of these privileges, which I shall later develop at leisure from their different points of view.

1. He was the worthy spouse of Our Lady, if indeed any spouse could be worthy of her; for the Holy Trinity in designing him for such an honour, endowed him with all the qualities necessary for bearing that name with dignity and propriety. And as this glorious title is, so to speak, the original source or root from which proceeded all the glories of St. Joseph, St. Matthew considered he could say nothing higher of him than call him *Spouse of Mary.*

2. He was the supposed father of Jesus Christ, and Our Lady did not hesitate to give him this title; thus when she found the Child Jesus in the temple, she said to Him: 'Thy father and I have sought Thee sorrowing.'

3. He was the representative of God the Father, Who, in communicating to him the honour of paternity to the Incarnate Word, willed that he should call Him by the name of

son, a name which He alone gives in heaven to the Uncreated Word. Thus God Who formerly had said He would give His glory to no one, now, by an exceptional favour communicates, in a manner, to a mortal that paternity which is the special glory of the Eternal Father. What is still more, God, according to St. John Damascene and St. Bernard, in giving to Joseph the name of father, gave him also a father's heart—that is, the authority, the solicitude, and the love of a father.

4. Joseph was also the representative of the Holy Ghost, Who confided to him the Virgin Mary, placing His spouse under Joseph's dependence and direction. Great God! what a favour! The Father and the Holy Ghost intrust to him what is most dear to them! To what sublimity of virtue must he have attained to acquit himself worthily of such a charge!

5. Our Lady, in giving him her hand, gave him also her whole heart. Never did a wife love her husband so tenderly, so ardently, nor revere him more profoundly. Mary and Joseph, says St. Bernardin of Siena, were

but one heart and soul; they were two in one same mind, one same affection, and each of them was the other's second self, because Our Lady and he were, so to speak, only one person. The heart of Mary with that of Joseph, and the heart of Joseph with that of Mary, who ever could imagine a union so intimate, a grace so great !

6. Joseph was the superior of Jesus and Mary, whose submission to him was so complete as to enrapture the Angels. Those pure spirits tremble in heaven before the infinite majesty of the great God ; what must they have thought when they saw Joseph command the little Jesus as a father, and the Divine Infant disport Himself on the breast of Joseph, like a bee in the bosom of a lily ! As for the Queen of the world, as she had vowed, so she rendered to her chaste spouse all possible respect and obedience, never considering him otherwise, says Gerson, than as her lord and master. What a dignity to be the master of that Virgin more noble than the Seraphim !

7. He it was who nourished Jesus and Mary. A true father to that family, he gained their

bread by the labour of his hands, and the sweat of his brow. He led them into Egypt, acting in this mystery as the representative of the Most Holy Trinity. What an honour to nourish Him Who nourishes the whole world, to give bread to Him Who covers our fields with plentiful harvests!

8. He is called by the Abbot Rupert Guardian of the Child Jesus. Without an earthly father, his Divine Ward cast Himself into the arms of Joseph, His only protector, defender and support.

9. He was also the treasurer of the Saviour, and of Joseph more than of any other may it be said : ' Blessed is the faithful and wise servant, whom God has established as grand master of His family, to whose hands He has committed all His treasures, the government of all His possessions.' What confidence does not this office imply!

10. We do not hesitate to say that Joseph was the Saviour of the Saviour. Joseph, son of Jacob, was called the Saviour of the world, and he was not only the type, in the first place, of Jesus Christ, but also of St. Joseph, who had the honour of preserving the Divine Infant

from the fury of Herod. As Our Lord deserves the name of Saviour of man, because He preserves man from eternal death, so it is allowable to call St. Joseph Saviour of the Saviour, because he preserved Him from temporal death. Glorious Saint to whom were entrusted the person of the Incarnate Word, and all the secrets of the Eternal Father! The Angel might himself have carried the Child into Egypt ; but not daring to do so, he came as the messenger of Heaven and of God Himself, to Joseph who was chosen for that employment.

11. To these titles add another distinguished title, that of having been the Master of his Master. Jesus was like an apprentice in the workshop of Joseph, who taught him to work as a carpenter, so that everyone said of Jesus: 'Is not this the carpenter's son, a carpenter Himself ? Have we not often seen Him handling the plane and the chisel, helping His father Joseph ?' What must St. Joseph have thought when he saw his divine apprentice, taking pains at His work—He Who by a single word had created the universe !

12. Joseph was the presumptive heir of Jesus Christ, and of Our Lady, since the father then naturally inherited from his son, and the husband from his wife. What an incomparable advantage!

13. In all orders of things great privileges are attached to being the eldest, the first. The first Apostle, the first Martyr, the first Seraph, the first son of the Patriarchs, all have special rights which belong to no others; therefore I conclude that St. Joseph has singular prerogatives above all other men, for he was the first to contemplate the admirable humanity of Our Lord Jesus, the first to adore Him, the first to touch Him, the first to serve Him, to nourish Him, and to dwell with Him, the first to hear Him speak and to be enlightened by His divine instructions. He is the first confessor for the faith, since he first suffered for the love of Jesus Christ, forsaking his home and his country to fly with Him; the first Apostle making the Messias known to men, by announcing Him in Egypt; the first man, perhaps, who made profession and vow of virginity, and kept it in the state of marriage; in a word, the first Christian and the first model for the children of the Church. All these distinctions give Joseph great pre-eminence over all other Saints, and are almost infinite, so that we may apply to him what Jacob said of his eldest son Reuben : 'Excelling (his brethren) in gifts, greater in command.'*

14. Theologians teach that the office of St. Joseph was more exalted than any other in the Church. We do not speak of Our Lady, who is always above all comparison. They acknowledge, it is true, that in the ecclesiastical hierarchy, and in the order of sanctifying grace, the office of the Apostles is the most sublime ; but they recognise in the Mother of God, and in St. Joseph, an order, a hierarchy apart, that of the hypostatic union, destined to the immediate service of the person of the Word made flesh, and this second hierarchy is superior in dignity to the first.† The Apostles, as we said above, are only the servants of Jesus Christ ; Mary and Joseph are His mother and His father.

But shall I be able to relate all that God has

---

* 'Prior in donis, major in imperio' (Gen. xlix. 3).
† Suarez, *De Incarnat.*, p. 2, disp. 8, sect. 1.

done for St. Joseph? No; I plainly confess that there is neither mind, nor pen, nor tongue capable of imagining, writing, or expressing the grandeur and incomparable prerogatives of this spouse of the Virgin, this father of Jesus Christ, this governor of both! And yet, speak I must! Pardon, O great Saint, my unpardonable boldness! Yet, if your holy spouse, Our Lady, will deign to inspire me with a part of what she knows, if she will give fluency to my pen and warmth to my heart, I shall be able to say enough to content your pious clients, and edify your faithful servants.

CHAPTER III.

THE NATURAL GIFTS OF ST. JOSEPH.

It is a fundamental law of the household of God, that when the Almighty makes choice of a man to accomplish any great work, He endows him with all the graces necessary to acquit himself with dignity and perfection of the office confided to him by infallible Providence. This principle is laid down by the Angelical Doctor, and is borrowed by him from St. Paul.* Now, the Holy Trinity had from all eternity destined St. Joseph to be the spouse of the Mother of God, and the supposed father of the little Saviour, and to fulfil towards Him all the obligations of real paternity: hence it follows that St. Joseph was endowed with all

---

* 'Unicuique Deus dat gratiam proportionatam ei ad quod eligitur' (S. Thom., *In Epist. ad Rom.*, cap. viii., lect. 5).—'Idoneos nos fecit ministros Novi Testamenti' (2 Cor. iii. 6).

that was necessary for this double office. Oh that I were eloquent enough to give you a faint idea of the qualities necessary to be the worthy spouse of the Queen of Angels, the adopted father of the King of earth and heaven! Truly, in him, as St. Gregory of Nazianzen says of St. Basil, nature had transformed itself into grace?

A Greek author said that he was tempted to believe in Pythagoras' system of the transmigration of souls, because it seemed to him that all beautiful souls had returned to earth to animate the body of this philosopher. This, indeed, was rashly and foolishly spoken. But we may truly say that all natural and moral virtues seem to have united their efforts to embellish the person of the great St. Joseph, and to enrich his soul.

When the first Joseph drove out of the palace of Pharaoh in a royal chariot, Scripture tells us that the people pressed around as he passed, to contemplate the magnificence of his person, and the beauty of his countenance. Indeed, Joseph appeared to be more like an angel than like a man. Now, St. Bernard establishes a parallel between the two Josephs, which is entirely to the advantage of the second; and this cannot surprise us, because the latter, being appointed to an office infinitely more honourable than that of the former, must consequently possess far superior qualities and virtues. What virginal modesty appeared in his venerable countenance! what sweetness in his eyes! what gravity in his words! what wisdom and discernment in the manner he governed God's family, composed of only two persons, but whose value outweighed that of all creation!

When it pleases the King of kings to call a man to authority, He imprints on his brow a character of majesty which commands respect and obedience. We read in the first Book of Kings, that in the tribe of Benjamin there was a man called Cis. He had a son named Saul, 'a chosen and goodly man, and there was not among the children of Israel a goodlier person than he; from his shoulders and upward he appeared above all the people.' Such was the man whom God chose to be the first king of the Jewish nation. Tell me, then, what must have been the majesty of Joseph, to whom was given authority over the King and the Queen of the universe ?

In the genealogy of Joseph, St. Matthew shows him to be descended in a direct line from fourteen patriarchs, beginning with Abraham, until David ; from fourteen kings after David, until the transmigration of the Jews to Babylon ; and from fourteen princes or chiefs of the people, after the transmigration of Babylon, until Jesus Christ. Why did the Holy Spirit inspire this long enumeration ? Doubtless, among other reasons, to show that the descendant of so many great men was also the heir of their noble qualities and royal virtues. All the perfections distributed among so many princes were united in St. Joseph. The liberal hand of the Creator poured forth in profusion all qualities of body and soul upon this great Saint, so as to make him worthy of espousing the Queen of Angels and men, of being the supposed father of the little Messias, and of being teacher of the divine apprentice, Who, during eighteen years, deigned to work under his direction in the humble workshop at Nazareth.

Were we to question the most holy Virgin

about the graces of her spouse, she would, no doubt, reply in words borrowed from the Canticles : ' My beloved spouse is white as snow by his virginal purity, red as scarlet by his modesty ; chosen out of thousands. His head is as the finest gold ; his eyes as doves upon brooks of waters which are washed with milk and set beside the plentiful streams ; his hands shine like gold, full of the precious stones of all good works ; his voice is full of sweetness ; all the graces of nature are united in his face ; he is beloved of heaven and earth.'

To this portrait we shall only add one word, which Mary could not say, but which St. Bernardin has said for her. Joseph was the living image of his virgin spouse ; they resembled each other like two pearls. Tell me what was the beauty of Mary, and I shall tell you what was that of Joseph. But we would do great injustice to our glorious Patriarch were we to imagine that his resemblance to his most chaste spouse was merely outward. 'All the glory of the King's daughter is within.'*
This may also be said of St. Joseph, as we shall see in the following chapters.

* ' Omnis gloriæ jus filiæ Regis ab intus ' (Ps. xliv. 14).

CHAPTER IV.

ALL natural gifts are not to be compared in value to the value of one supernatural grace. What must then be the wealth of St. Joseph's soul! The graces without number which he received from divine generosity are so stupendous that our feeble minds are unable to comprehend them, and it seems to me not to be one of the least glories of Our Lady to have had as spouse a man whom the hand of the Almighty had endowed with every virtue. For my part, I desire to lose myself in the incomprehensible grandeur of this great Saint, and after I have said all that can be said, to confess humbly that I have said nothing. For if it be true, as I have already established, that God apportions His gifts in proportion to the offices He imposes on man, so

28

that he may support them with dignity, St. Joseph must have received such a prodigious abundance of heavenly graces that we cannot contemplate them without holy fear. We shall now return to what we briefly alluded to in the first chapters, and shall derive therefrom conclusions very glorious for our Saint.

I.—*St. Joseph, virgin.*

In the first place, he was a virgin, so much that his virginal purity yielded in brilliancy and merit to that of the Queen of Virgins alone. What supreme graces he must have received to preserve this angelical virtue in an age which despised virginity, and to guard this delicate lily without the slightest taint or stain on its brilliant whiteness! According to the holy Fathers, he that preserves intact the treasure of virginity ranks higher than the Angels. To what a degree of holiness must not St. Joseph have attained, who was the first to preserve it in the state of marriage, and preserved it with such fidelity!

II.—*St. Joseph, guardian angel of Mary.*

Secondly, Joseph was chosen from all eternity to be the visible guardian angel of the virginity of Our Lady. Must not, then, his soul have been armed with every virtue, and fortified by every assistance necessary for such a noble and admirable office ? Consider what manner of man Joseph is ! The Angels and Saints are only the servants of the glorious Virgin, while he is her guardian angel and her spouse. This title, to which we now only allude in passing, is far beyond the comprehension of our feeble intelligence ; for, husband and wife being but one heart and one soul, what must be the sovereign dignity of a man who, so to speak, is one with the most holy Mother of the living God !

St. Bernardin of Siena has boldly grasped this thought. He says that as the virginal marriage of Mary and Joseph consisted in the union of their wills, the friendship of their hearts, and the love of their souls increased to such a degree that there never were two hearts more completely identified, two souls more dissolved into one, and he adds that the Holy

Spirit would never have formed this union
without rendering the husband perfectly
similar to the wife.* It was beseeming that
the likeness of these two suns should be so
striking, that it would be difficult to dis-
tinguish one from the other. On one hand,
the holiness of Our Lady outshines the holiness of all creatures; on the other hand, the
holiness of Joseph is entirely alike the holiness of Mary. Later on we shall treat this
subject more at length.

III.—*St. Joseph, guardian of Jesus.*

Let us dwell a little on this title, 'guardian
of Jesus,' so as to understand the eminence of
St. Joseph's dignity. The learned and pious
Rupert, of the Order of St. Benedict, says
Jacob's ladder is a figure of the genealogy of
Jesus Christ: the different steps being the
patriarchs, the kings, the princes, his ancestors,
and the upmost step being St. Joseph, who

* 'Quomodo cogitare potest mens discreta, quod
Spiritus Sanctus tanta unione uniret menti tantæ
Virginis aliquam animam, nisi ei virtutum operatione
simillimam?' (*Serm. de S. Joseph*, art. 2, c. i.)

stands with open arms to receive and embrace
the Infant Messias, the divine pupil, to Whom
he must serve as guardian and father.* To
understand the importance of this office we
must remember the words of St. Paul : ' As
long as the heir is a child he differeth nothing
from a servant, though he be lord of all ; but
is under tutors and governors until the time
appointed by the father.'† Meanwhile his
possessions and his person are disposed of
without consulting him, and when the time
of his majority arrives the master ratifies all,
as if it had been done by himself.

Oh, reader, can you imagine such pre-
eminence as that of St. Joseph ? Our Lord
said : ' Blessed is the faithful and wise servant,
for the Lord will place him over all His
goods.' What power ! to have everything in
his hands ; to be accountable to no one ! I

---

* ' Supremus scalæ gradus, cui Dominus innixus est,
iste est beatus Joseph, vir Mariæ, de qua Jesus qui
vocatur Christus natus est. Quomodo iste Deus et
Dominus huic innixus est ? Utique tanquam tutori
pupillus, quippe qui in hoc mundo sine patre natus est,
ita innixus est huic beato Joseph, ut esset infantulo
iste pater optimus ; ut hujus solatio paterno puer cum
Virgine puerpera sustentaretur ' (in Matth., *De gloria
et honore Filii hominis*, cap. i.).

† Gal. iv. 1, 2.

wish I were equal to the task of treating this sublime subject and showing the significance of these words: 'He has placed him over all His goods?' He is general administrator of all the goods of the Incarnate Word, with full power to distribute them to whom and when he pleases. Nay, as governor of His person, he can give God Himself to whom he pleases! Is not this to be exalted above men and Angels, and even, to a certain extent, above God Himself?

Consider now what follows from this with regard to the sanctity of Joseph. Since it was in his power to distribute the goods of Jesus to whom he would, can you doubt that he took for himself an abundance of all that was most precious?

When the Saviour traversed the towns and villages of Judea, it sufficed to touch the hem of His garment in order to receive signal graces. My God, my Creator, with what innumerable graces must not Joseph have been enriched from the heart of the Divine Child, Whom he carried so often in his arms, lavishing on Him his kisses and caresses! When Jesus slept on the breast of

33

the holy Patriarch, can you doubt that He
communicated to him the sweetest and most
ineffable graces ? Perhaps He went to sleep in
his arms, with the intention, while reposing on
his breast, to communicate to him His favours,
and to crown him with His mercies. If it be
Paradise to contemplate the Eternal and Uncreated Word in the bosom of His father, is
it not likewise Paradise to see the Word made
flesh, now on the virginal bosom of Mary
His mother, and now in the arms of His
foster-father Joseph ?

IV.—*Joseph living in the company of Jesus
and Mary.*

Lastly, I say, that St. Joseph, true mirror
of virginal purity, guardian angel of Our
Lady, and protector of Jesus Christ, had the
incomparable happiness of living, according
to the general belief, twenty-five years in their
sweet and holy company, and of having constantly before his eyes these models of perfection.

From all parts of the Christian world the
pious faithful travel to St. Mary Major in

Rome, to Loretto, to Montserrat, and other places of pilgrimage, where it pleases God to manifest the goodness and the power of His most holy Mother. These pious pilgrims feel the greatest confidence. They do not doubt that, praying humbly before the picture of Mary, painted by St. Luke, or before other images of Our Lady, honoured in these sanctuaries, they will obtain all they ask for. But the chapel of Loretto was the house and ordinary habitation of Joseph, who needed not to make pilgrimages, or to seek for pictures and copies, having the original continually before his eyes. There he conversed sweetly with Mary, and recommended himself to her holy prayers. There she, who never rejects the least of her servants, certainly denied nothing to him. Think of what blessings the presence of such a spouse must have imparted to the heart of Joseph: while she looked at him, inflaming him with the kindling rays of her burning charity; while her blessed lips addressed him with words that might have entranced the hearts of men and of Angels, nay, of God Himself. As the devout pilgrim never fails to find Jesus in the sanctuaries of Mary; so, in the house of Nazareth, Joseph had Jesus always present with Mary, and saw, with his eyes, the Divine Child grow in age, in wisdom, and in grace, before God and men.

Who can describe what superabundance of divine blessings inundated the soul of this incomparable Saint ! He, too, every day, and every moment, grew in grace and in virtue, enjoying without interruption what we may call the beatific vision, never ceasing to see God, and to be seen by Him. To see God, and to be regarded by Him cannot fail to produce a blessing, can never be without fruit. The burning rays of the sun gild all that is exposed to them ; Jesus Christ, the sun of Paradise, Our Lady, the star of the Church, were as the planets which favoured Joseph with their beneficent aspect, the sacred channels through which God the Father exerted His influence ; how, then, could the soul of the great Patriarch fail to be illuminated with the splendours of the Saints, to overflow with the treasures of Divinity ?

In ancient times, had one asked why a mine of gold or silver was to be found in one place, pearls and diamonds in others ;

here, flowers of exquisite beauty, and there, fragrant balm; the answer would have been given, without more research, that a secret influence from heaven smiled upon that favoured land. Now, the eyes of the Eternal Father were ever resting on St. Joseph; the Holy Spirit was continually abiding in his soul; Jesus Christ regarded him with the love of a son; Our Lady's affection for him was unbounded; the Angels were devoted to him. How is it possible to imagine or describe the graces of this heart, the heavenly blessings in the most pure soul of this peerless man?

Our Lord has said that if anyone love Him, he will be loved by the Father, and that both will come and make their abode in the breast of that man. Never was this promise verified more completely than in the innocent heart of Joseph, who, besides the general love common to all the servants of Jesus Christ, enjoyed the special love due to a guardian, a governor, a master, and a father.

Great were also the graces which Joseph derived from his constant communion with his most holy spouse. His eyes were always directed towards her and Jesus, studying their conduct, imitating, so to speak, their every action. He treasured up in his heart all the eminent perfections which he observed in theirs. Open the heart of Joseph, and you will find therein the faithful copies, the perfect imitations of the sublime virtues of his adopted son Jesus, and of his blessed spouse Mary. The hands of those who always work with balm become as odoriferous as if they themselves were made of balm.

I wish I could give as a fact what I have read in certain ancient authors, that nature has formed diamonds which, when exposed to the sun, emit rays so piercing, that they have the virtue of changing a piece of crystal into a diamond nearly as precious as themselves. Yet that which, in the order of nature, is but fiction, is found to be true in the order of grace. Joseph, pure as crystal, and constantly exposed to the rays emanating from Jesus and Mary, was as if transformed into a most excellent copy of the celestial beauties of both. O ineffable transformation ! O new trinity of persons, and unity of hearts ! Pardon me, great and amiable Saint, if I dare to speak of what is inexpressible; if I attempt to develop a part of your greatness. Enlighten my mind, fortify my heart, that I may proceed with a firm and unerring step on the path of thy praises.

CHAPTER V.

THE prophet Isaias says that the time shall come when, delivering a book to a man that is learned, one shall say to him, Read this; and he shall answer, I cannot, for it is sealed.* Whatever may be the signification of this mysterious book, does it not present to us a glorious image of St. Joseph? God the Father wrote in his heart, as in a book, all the secrets of the Incarnation and of the hidden life of the Word made flesh; but this volume has remained so well sealed that, during many centuries, the most learned men in the Church knew almost nothing of the immense world of graces and wonders contained in it. St. Teresa of Jesus was one of the first to read in this book some of the

* Is. xxix. 11.

40

privileges of the holy spouse of Our Lady;
and this kindled in her heart a lively desire to
spread devotion to this great Patriarch among
all the faithful. Were it not for the seraphic
reformer of Carmel, St. Joseph might still
perhaps be little known, and be honoured by
only a few privileged souls.

Joseph himself it was who kept the book of
his own virtues sealed. He was so modest
and humble that he hid from the sight of
men the perfection of his actions, and
the treasures of his soul. His was to all
appearance but a common life. He spoke
so little that in the whole of the Gospels
you will not find one single word addressed
by him, either to Jesus, or to his spouse, or
to the Archangel Gabriel, or to any other
person in the world. He was like that place
in the Temple of Jerusalem, called the Holy
of Holies, of which nothing was visible but
the curtain concealing its glories. We are
thus reduced to divine all that is written in
this book, or to do like St. John, when, as he
tells us in the fifth chapter of the Apocalypse,
a similar book was presented to him. Being
unable to read it, he began to weep so much

41

that he excited the pity of the Angels and of
the Lamb, who opened for him the mysterious
book, and communicated to him all its secrets.
Alas! shall our devotion to this holy Patriarch
ever become so great that it shall move him
to compassion, and make him discover to us
all the secrets hidden in his heart? Meanwhile, reader, if you desire to understand
something of the glories of St. Joseph, you
will, I think, in the following considerations,
find the just measure by which to weigh
them.

I.—*First measure of the graces of St. Joseph:
the title of ' Father of Jesus.'*

The first measure by which to understand
the graces and sanctity of Joseph, is his title
of ' Father of Jesus.' Theologians teach that
the more nearly a man is destined by his
office to serve the Divine Person of the Incarnate Word, the more eminent must be the
graces given to him for the worthy perform-
ance of that office. In the first chapter of
the prophecy of Daniel, we read that the
young Israelites chosen for the immediate
service of King Nabuchodonosor, must be of

the 'king's seed, and of the princes, in whom there was no blemish, and well-favoured. . . . And the king appointed them daily provision of his own meat, and ·of the wine which he drank himself, that, being nourished three years, afterwards they might stand before the king.'* Now, after Our Lady, no human being has been called to serve the Lord Jesus so nearly as St. Joseph, consequently none has a larger share than he in the graces of the Eternal Father. The sacred humanity of the Saviour, being united hypostatically to the Divinity, has received a whole world of almost infinite graces; after Jesus comes His most holy Mother, who carried Him nine months in her virginal womb, and a thousand times in her arms; after Mary comes Joseph, the foster-father of Jesus, and the guardian of His adorable person. No other Saint was called to the immediate service of the Word made flesh; consequently no other has received from God gifts proportionate to the dignity of this office. I know well that, as St. Anselm says, the ministry of the Apostles is the highest in the Church, and that the title

* Dan. i. 3-5.

43

of Apostle is even greater than that of precursor of Jesus Christ; but I say with Suarez, that the ministry of St. Joseph is of an order still higher and more perfect, and that Our Lady and St. Joseph form a hierarchy apart, superior to all the orders of the other Saints in the Church of God.*

Who can understand how many graces were requisite to make St. Joseph worthy of the title of Father of Jesus, and to enable him to fulfil all its duties? So far as a man is capable of participating in the paternity of God the Father, so far was Joseph adorned and enriched with heavenly graces; and this implies such an amount of greatness, that God alone can know its weight and measure. If, in Solomon's Temple, which contained the Ark of the Covenant, everything was to be covered with gold, what graces must have gilded the soul, the heart, the breast of this holy man, the living throne of the living God, in whose arms reposed the Lord of all the Angels! That a man should go to 'sleep in the Lord' is indeed precious, but that God should go to sleep on the bosom of a man, surpasses all human comprehension.

* Suarez, *De Incarnat.*, p. 2, disp. 8, sect. 1.

Origen is of opinion that when Jesus said
to Mary, 'Woman, behold thy son,' His word
produced the effect that St. John became,
for His Mother, another Himself, as if He
had said: 'My Mother, behold your Jesus,
to Whom you gave birth.'* In the same
manner, when God the Father said to Jesus:
'My son, behold Joseph; he will be your father,'
it is as if He said: ' Joseph is for you, another
Myself.' And so it was; for, says Abbot
Rupert, at the same time that God formed
the body of His Son from the most pure blood
of the Virgin, He infused into the heart of
Joseph His own paternal love, in order that
the latter might be for the Incarnate Word
upon earth, what He Himself is to the Uncreated Word in eternity.† Now it is much
more glorious to be the adopted father of
Jesus Christ, than to be the adopted son of
Our Lady, whence it follows that we are
obliged to recognise in Joseph a dignity, not

* 'Perinde est ac si dixisset; Ecce hic est Jesus
quem genuisti' (*Commentar. in Joan.*, n. 6).
† ' De carne virginis hominem formans, paterno viro
huic, ejus qui nascebatur infantis amorem penitus in-
fudit' (in Matth., *De gloria et honore Filii hominis*,
lib. 1).

merely superior to that of the beloved disciple,
but an almost infinite dignity, since he is like
another Eternal Father in this world. The
Angel of the Schools does not hesitate to
call divine maternity an infinite dignity.*
Why, then, should we not say that the paternity of Joseph approaches the infinite, since,
after her who really is the Mother of God,
there is none greater than he to whom God
communicated His paternity, and whom Jesus
Christ many thousand times called by the
name of father? Thus, when the Infant God
said, 'My father,' one could not tell if He
spoke to God His Father, or to Joseph His
father. Oh, what happy equivocation! what
glorious parallel, by which Joseph is, in a
manner, compared to the Eternal Father,
in spite of the infinite distance there is
between them! Must not the heart of this
godlike man have been ready to burst in his
breast, to melt with tenderness, when, holding
the hand of the Infant Jesus, he said to Him,
'My Son;' or when the Divine Child, with
innocent flattery, named him His father?

* S. Thom., p. 1, q. 25, a. 6, ad 4.

What is the meaning of those words in Ecclesiasticus : 'God created man after His own image, and clothed him with strength according to Himself; adorning him with virtues and divine splendours' ?* Taking them literally, they are only an explanation of God's words in the first chapter of Genesis : ' Let us make man to our image and likeness.' Thus they apply to man in general, and consequently to each man, and we must allow that they incomparably exalt his dignity. Nevertheless, I believe that I enter into your thoughts, reader, when I apply them, in a special manner, to our glorious Patriarch. What man indeed was ever so well formed to the image and likeness of God the Father, as the adopted father of Jesus ? Do not you see in Joseph an image of God, a resemblance with God, which belongs alone to this friend of God, and is shared by no one else ? Nothing bears such a resemblance to the Father, with the Uncreated Word in His bosom, as Joseph, carrying the Incarnate Word in his arms and on his heart ! Jesus Christ, speaking of His

* Eccli. xvii. 2.

Heavenly Father, says : ' I and the Father are one.' These words we may apply to St. Joseph : he and Jesus are truly one. Since it is certain that Joseph participated in divine paternity, what an honour it is for him to have a union so intimate with God the Son, and with God the Father a communion of property in what is incommunicable ! Suppose for a moment that the Father and the Son had entered into a holy rivalry to adorn and enrich the heart and soul of St. Joseph. The Father wills that nothing shall be wanting to him who is to be the father of His Son. The Son would wish to give even more to him who is to be His father. Who will be the conqueror in this divine contest ? The Eternal Father or the Eternal Word ?

There is still another thought that strikes me. God the Father having chosen St. Joseph to govern His only Son in His place and in His name, well knew that without special assistance no mere mortal could acquit himself worthily of such a noble and difficult task. Therefore he took up his abode in the heart of Joseph in order personally to direct

His Son Jesus through the ministry of this man after His own heart. The Lord also commanded Moses to go before Pharao, saying: 'I will be in thy mouth, and I will teach thee what thou shalt speak.'* If God willed to be in the mouth of His servant Moses to speak with an earthly king, can you wonder that He should put Himself into the heart of Joseph in order to govern, along with him, His own Son? What a source of the most precious gifts must not this intimate presence of God the Father have been for the adopted father of Jesus! What an ocean of graces must He not have poured into that holy soul! What torrents of lights shed upon Joseph's mind! What fire kindled in his heart! and all this was done on account of the Infant Messias, Whom Joseph was called upon to direct, to defend, to nourish, and to instruct in all things.

* 'Perge igitur ; et ego ero in ore tuo doceboque te quid loquaris ' (Ex. iv. 12).

II.—*Second measure of the graces of St. Joseph : the title of 'Spouse of Mary.'*

The second measure of the graces and sanctity of St. Joseph is his dignity of Spouse of Our Lady. According to St. John Damascene the dignity of Spouse of Mary is one so elevated that no human eloquence can express it. Neither is it possible worthily to celebrate the greatness of St. Joseph without understanding that of his holy Spouse, who is the Queen of the Saints and the Angels, and the Mother of God. Who, then, is to form a true idea of the dignity of St. Joseph,* as also of the graces he holds in consequence of that dignity ?

St. Bernardin of Siena says that the

---

* According to the ancient law, whoever espouses a queen becomes king by the fact of his marriage : '*Nubentem reginæ consequens est regem fieri.*' From this, St. Leonard of Port Maurice draws the following conclusion : 'Mary is the Queen of Angels and of Saints ; Joseph is the Spouse of Mary, therefore he is also King of Angels and Saints ; and consequently it is allowable to invoke him by this title, notwithstanding that the Church has consecrated the custom of addressing this invocation principally to Jesus Christ.'—*St. Joseph d'après les Saints*, par le R. P. Marcel Bouix, c. xviii. (Note by the Editor.)

virginal marriage of Mary and Joseph was only contracted on earth after having been decided in heaven, and that these two spouses were perfectly worthy one of the other. Mary surpassed all men and Angels in the sovereign plenitude of her graces; therefore it was necessary that, after her, Joseph should be the most holy human being that existed, that had ever existed, or that should ever exist upon earth. Or is it possible to believe that heaven contains any servant of Mary more eminent in holiness than he who has the honour of being her spouse, her lord, and her master? And let us even suppose that Joseph had not been enriched with the most precious gifts of heaven before he espoused the most holy Virgin: what must she not afterwards have asked God for her spouse; what innumerable graces must not she have obtained for him! For if St. Bernard be right in asserting that no grace comes down from heaven to earth but through the munificent hands of the Mother of God; if there be no kind of celestial blessing which she has not obtained for one or the other of her servants; must we not believe that she will have done more for her spouse and the guardian angel of her virginity than for all other human beings ?

Here is a beautiful thought which I borrow from St. Gregory of Nazianzen, and which applies perfectly to our subject. This great Bishop tells us that his sister, St. Gorgonia, had a husband whom she loved like her own self; and knowing from the Holy Scriptures that husband and wife are not two, but one, she desired ardently that her husband should serve the Lord as she herself did, lest she should find herself constrained to belong to God only by halves. Now, there never were two hearts, two souls more united than those of Mary and Joseph ; nor could this faithful Virgin ever remain satisfied with rendering half service to God. Therefore she used every endeavour that her other half, St. Joseph, should be supremely exalted in all sorts of perfections. To use St. Gregory's own words, she intensely desired that her spouse should be perfect, in order that no part of herself should remain imperfect.* Certainly Mary

* 'Cupiebat ut maritus quoque perficeretur, ne ipsius aliquid imperfectum relinqueretur' (*Orat. in laudem sororis suæ Gorgoniæ*).

did everything to secure this object: she sighed, she prayed. And can you believe that Jesus could refuse anything which His tender Mother asked for His beloved father? Each day, then, the treasure of graces in Joseph's soul visibly grew; each day his sanctity increased, and the charity of his heart grew more ardent. What, indeed, could he not hope for, having His spouse as advocate, His son as arbitrator, and God the Father as protector!

Such then are the two principal titles by which we must measure the graces and sanctity of Joseph. Such are the two plenteous sources, or rather the two majestic rivers which watered and enriched His soul. Never shall we fully understand the perfections of the adopted father of Jesus, the holy Spouse of Mary.

CHAPTER VI.

IT would be difficult, if not impossible, to deduce all the consequences of the two august titles which are the glory of St. Joseph, and the source and measure of his sanctity. We shall therefore only treat of those which seem to us the most glorious, and which present themselves most naturally to our mind.

I.—*First consequence: Jesus and Mary belong to St. Joseph, as well their persons as their goods.*

Ancient laws lay down clearly that if a treasure be discovered in a house or in a field, it belongs, by right, to the proprietor of the house or of the ground. This law gives great advantages to the glorious St. Joseph, for the Incarnation took place in his house, now the chapel of Loretto. There it was that his most holy spouse became the Mother of God, some months after their espousals; hence the treasure of God made man, the ineffable mysteries, the torrents of grace, which were found in his house, and in his spouse, belong by a double title to St. Joseph, as legitimate owner of both.

Divine law agrees with human law. 'Thou shalt be under thy husband's power,' God said to Eve, 'and he shall have dominion over thee;* and all that is thine shall belong to him.' Truly, if the person of the wife be not in her own power, independently of her husband, much less is all the rest. Now, according to St. Bonaventure, all the treasure of God, and of the Angels, all the wealth of Paradise, was in the soul of Our Lady,† and consequently at the disposal of her holy spouse. She loved to say to him: 'O Joseph!

---

* 'Sub viri potestate eris, et ipse dominabitur tui' (Gen. iii. 16).

† 'Ager est Maria, in qua thesaurus Angelorum, imo totus Dei Patris absconditus est' (S. Bonavent., *In Speculo B.M.V.*, lect. 7).

the Almighty has done great things in me; in me, who am lowliness itself, He has shown the riches of His mercy. Help my soul to glorify the Lord, and to render to Him the thanks-givings which are His due; for all I have received from His infinite munificence belongs to you; "all I have is thine."* And this communion of goods was so absolute, that all which belonged to the one belonged to the other; if indeed we should not rather say that the husband was still more master of all than the wife.

II.—*Second consequence : Joseph has the right of commanding Jesus and Mary.*

This proposition is so clear, that there is no need to prove it; and the few words I shall speak on the subject are not so much to establish the fact, as sweetly to occupy our minds and hearts with this admirable privilege of St. Joseph.

Let us boldly apply to this holy Patriarch what Cardinal St. Peter Damian says of the Queen of Heaven : Mary does not merely

* ' Omnia mea tua sunt' (Luc xv. 31).

56

request, she commands ; for she is lady
and mistress, not servant.* Joseph also
can, if he please, command his spouse, and
dispose absolutely of her person and her property. ' Do this,' he can say ; ' give me that !
for I command you by the power given me by
God over you, and by the laws of our legitimate marriage.' It is true that this holy man
was so humble, and had such veneration for
his spouse, that he never exerted his right of
commanding. The good ask what they might
command, while fools command instead of ask-
ing. But as Mary considered in her heart that
it was God Who had given her Joseph as spouse,
she looked up to him with entire submission,
and anticipated his wishes with tender love.

Yet Joseph was to enjoy still a higher
prerogative. The Uncreated Word, by taking
our nature in the womb of the ever-blessed
Virgin, chose to bind Himself to render
her honour, service, and obedience ; and
Joseph being the spouse and master of
Mary, it follows that Jesus could not be
dependent on His Mother without, at the

* 'Non solum rogans, sed imperans ; domina, non
ancilla' (S. Petr. Damian., *Serm.* 44. *In Nativ. B.M.V.*).

same time, being dependent on him who was her lord and master. How beautiful it is to see a mortal command two persons who are worthy to rule in heaven and on earth ! How admirable to see those two persons whom the celestial hierarchies revere, cbey the slightest desire of an humble artisan, who gains his bread by the sweat of his brow !

Iphicrates, a celebrated Athenian general, was once asked by an orator what he was, to have such a high idea of himself. 'Are you a horse or a foot soldier ? Do you use the bow or the shield ?' Iphicrates replied : 'I am none of those of whom you speak ; but I command them all.'* Oh how justly these words may be applied to St. Joseph ! In his humility, he repeats that he is nothing, that he has nothing, that he can do nothing ; and yet, we may say with truth that Jesus and Mary are under obedience to Joseph ; that all they do is by Joseph's desire ; that their treasures are the treasures of Joseph ; since it is certain that the property of this son and of this spouse were at the disposal of the father of the family.

* Plutarc. Apophthegm., *De Iphicrate.*

III.—*Third consequence : Joseph has the right of being honoured by Jesus and Mary.*

Let us consider, in the third place, how, as father and spouse, this incomparable Saint has a right to be honoured by Jesus and Mary, since it is a precept, both natural and divine, that every son must honour his father, every wife her husband. Here Gerson expresses a sweet and loving thought; in the same way, he says, as Sara, according to the Holy Scriptures, called Abraham her lord, so also the Blessed Virgin, penetrated with respectful love for her spouse, gave him no other name than that of lord and master.* And what is still more, Joseph was such in very deed, having absolute command and disposal of her, and of her Son. The very love which I bear to Our Lady, makes me long to have Joseph for my good master also, since he is hers ; I desire to honour Joseph, because Mary honours him. Yes, I will praise and honour Joseph, because, according to a pious author, whoever praises and honours Joseph, praises

* Epistola de festo sancti Joseph celebrando.

and honours the Blessed Virgin also. For, as they are one in heart, in love, and in soul, the honours paid to the one are equally accepted by the other. Indeed, one feels inclined to believe that the humility of Our Lady is so extreme, her love so disinterested and so pure, that it pleases her more to see her beloved spouse honoured, than to be honoured herself. I know, at least, that she once deigned to thank St. Teresa for the honour that her zeal had procured to St. Joseph throughout the world.

But whilst Mary addresses her holy spouse by the name of lord, listen to the divine voice of the Infant Jesus calling him : ' My father, My father.' And this not once, but a hundred times a day. It seems to me, that, were the Seraphim capable of jealousy, they would feel a holy envy of this blessed Patriarch ; since it is their highest glory to be the servants of Jesus and of Mary, whose lord and father Joseph is. While, beyond the firmament, those transcendent spirits are prostrate before the throne of God, and tremble at His feet, they behold Jesus and Mary on earth, expecting and receiving the orders of Joseph, with a submission and humility which transport the Angels with admiration.

You have read in the Book of Esther how king Assuerus recompensed the fidelity of Mardochai. He commanded that he should be clothed with the king's apparel, and set upon the horse which the king was used to ride upon, and have the royal crown upon his head ; and that the first of the king's princes should hold his horse, and, going through the streets of the city, proclaim before him : 'Thus shall he be honoured, whom the king hath a mind to honour.' Something similar was done by God with regard to St. Joseph, with the essential difference, however, that God honours as God, while man can only honour as a man.

CHAPTER VII.

We may safely assert that St. Joseph
possessed, in a superior degree, all the graces
which we admire in the other Saints. The
following pages will establish this assertion
and thereby materially strengthen our devotion to this glorious Patriarch.

I.—*St. Joseph and the Saints of the Old
Testament.*

How much happier was St. Joseph, the last
of the Patriarchs, than all those who pre-
ceded him! Moses desired ardently to contemplate the divine Face of the Messias, and
he was obliged to wait fifteen centuries before
enjoying this happiness for an instant on
Mount Thabor. Abraham saw in spirit the
day of the coming of the Saviour upon earth,

and this vision, which passed like a flash of lightning, transported him with joy. How many kings, princes, pontiffs, and prophets longed to see, if only for one instant, this Desired of the nations, and to prostrate themselves in adoration before Him; yet never could they obtain this grace! And behold, Joseph carries Him in his arms, calls Him his Son, hears himself called father by the Infant God. 'When I saw the vision of the likeness of the glory of the Lord,' says the Prophet Ezechiel, 'I fell upon my face.' St. John writes: 'I saw one like to the Son of Man, and when I had seen Him I fell at His feet as dead.' Scripture says: 'No man shall see God and live. I have seen God; I must die.'* Yet Joseph sees the Incarnate God face to face. He sees Him every day, and each moment of the day, and he does not die either of fear or of love, or let us rather say, he dies of love; but the love which kills also resuscitates him. The same flames make him die, and bring him again to life.

* Ez. iii. 1.—Ap. i. 13, 17.—Ex. xxxiii. 20.—Jud. xiii. 22.

II.—*St. Joseph and the Apostle St. Peter.*

It is true that St. Peter received from Jesus Christ most extensive powers. Firstly, Christ gave him the keys of heaven, with power to open it, and, when necessary, to shut it; secondly, He commanded him to feed His sheep and His lambs; thirdly, He gave him the care of the whole Church, and the title of Vicar of Christ. 'Thou art Peter, and upon this rock I will build My Church;'* fourthly, he had the honour of loving Jesus Christ more tenderly than the others, and of wishing to defend Him at the risk of his life; fifthly, he was the first whose feet the Saviour washed, the first whom He consecrated bishop, in giving him His most precious body. But are all those favours to be compared with those granted by Heaven to St. Joseph?

In the first place, it is true that the keys of heaven were not given to him as to St. Peter: the keys are given to servants. But to Joseph, the spouse of the mother, the adopted father of the Son, not merely the keys, but

* 'Tu es Petrus, et super hanc petram ædificabo Ecclesiam meam' (Matt. xvi. 18).

the doors themselves are confided: since we may truly say that Jesus and Mary are the two living gates of Paradise. The Saviour gives Himself this name: 'I am the door of the sheep,'* and the Church gives the same to Our Lady: ' Gate of Heaven, pray for us.' Now, Joseph has the care of those gates; he is their guardian, and opens or shuts them according to his pleasure, which is that of God.

In the second place, it is not Joseph who is commanded as a simple shepherd to feed the lambs and the sheep; but to him it was given to nourish the Shepherd and the Shepherdess themselves; to feed the Lamb of God, and the Mother of this Divine Lamb. St. Peter distributes their food to the servants; but it is Joseph who must provide for the Infant Lord Jesus, and for the great Mistress of heaven and earth, the Blessed Virgin Mary.

In the third place, if St. Peter is the head of the Church, St. Joseph is the head of Jesus and of Mary, who are more precious in the eyes of God than the entire Church. Simon Peter is also the Vicar of Jesus Christ; but I shall show you presently that Joseph has been

* ' Ego sum ostium ovium ' (Joan. x. 7).

the vicar of each of the three Persons of the most Holy Trinity.

In the fourth place, when Jesus Christ asked St. Peter if the love he bore Him was greater than that of the other disciples, St. Joseph was not present; and my heart tells me that the Saviour would not have asked this question in the presence of Joseph, or that had He done so, St. Peter would have been eager to transfer the honour to him who incontestably merited it.

In the fifth place, Jesus once washed St. Peter's feet; but how often must not the same Saviour have rendered similar services to Joseph during the five and twenty years that He was subject to him!* Also, it was not one single time that He gave Himself to Joseph, but every day, and a thousand times a day.

Lastly, He made him, in a certain sense, Bishop of the Holy Family, and though his diocese was only composed of two persons, those two persons, in themselves, were worth more than all heaven and earth.

---

* 'Nemo ambigat Dominum Jesum, cum adhuc in puerili esset ætate, obsequia præstitisse Mariæ, ipsique Joseph' (S. Laurent. Justin., *Lib. de Obedientia*, c. viii.).

III.—*St. Joseph and the Apostle of the Gentiles.*

What shall we say of the great St. Paul, whose parallel is to be found nowhere? Truly, there is so much that is sublime in this Apostle, that, according to St. John Chrysostom, he has no equal. How glorious to have been surrounded with light from heaven on the way to Damascus, to have heard the voice of Jesus, to have spoken with Him! Was not he rapt even to the third heaven, where he heard secret ineffable words? Was not he armed with the sword of the Divine Word, and did not he announce this holy Word to the Gentiles, to the kings, and to the children of Israel? Lastly, did he not confirm all he taught by his patience, by his miracles, by his blood? Nothing can be more glorious, I own; but the stars, however brilliant, are eclipsed before the sun.

St. Joseph, it is true, was not caught up to heaven; but heaven descended into his house. He was not brought before the throne of God as a servant before his master; but the Incarnate Word was brought to Joseph, as a son to his kind father. Joseph did not see God for a moment like St. Paul, who knew not if it were in the body or out of the body, and who could repeat nothing of all that was said to him; but he was rapt in body and in soul during whole years; we may say, indeed, that his whole life was one continued ecstasy, one perpetual vision of God. Also he was quite able to repeat what he had heard, for he often spoke of it with his spouse, and together they held sweet and sublime conferences about all that Jesus had said to one or the other. Doubtless, few persons were capable of understanding those divine discourses; scarcely any besides Jesus, Mary, and Joseph. To St. Paul was revealed what an Apostle and a servant might know, but the secrets of a son to his father and mother were reserved for Mary and for Joseph.

IV.—*St. Joseph, St. John the Baptist and St. John the Apostle.*

Most certainly these two Saints were greatly favoured by the Lord Jesus. The one reposed upon the Heart of his Master during the Last Supper; the other poured the water of Jordan upon His divine Head, and, pointing Him out to heaven and earth, said : 'Behold the Lamb of God !' For these reasons, I avow that they received from the Lord most special graces, and were exalted, not merely above ordinary men, but also above the greatest Saints.

Yet, higher still than these two great servants of God, must we exalt him upon whom their Master bestowed the name of father. They cannot claim to be preferred before the father of the family. A thousand times did this happy Patriarch press the Infant Jesus to his heart ; a thousand times did he kiss the sacred breast, seat of the Divinity. He did not pour the water of Jordan on His Head one single time ; but how many times may he have moistened that Head with tears of joy and tenderness, when receiving Him from the hands of Our Lady and pressing Him to his bosom !

V.—*St. Joseph and the holy Angels.*

I know well that St. Michael was the valiant defender of the Incarnate Word, and that he overthrew Lucifer, who dared to dispute with the Man-God the honours of Divinity. But

I know, also, that Joseph saved the same
Incarnate Word from the fury of Herod, who
hoped to involve Him in the massacre of the
Innocents. He exposed his own life to save
that of the Infant Jesus, to preserve Him Who
was to work the salvation of the world by
dying on the Cross.

Much, indeed, do we owe to St. Gabriel for
the part he took in the work of the Incarnation, and for the good tidings of great joy
which he brought from heaven to earth. That
is true; but is not St. Bernard right when he
affirms that Joseph was, during his whole life,
the faithful co-operator of God in this great
mystery?* Gabriel had only to give the
orders; Joseph, to execute them, must en-
counter labours, journeys, dangers, and terrors.

The Angels came and ministered to the
Saviour in the dread solitude of the desert;
but that was only once, and they were in
great number; it cost them little, or rather
nothing to do so. But Joseph, during years,
laboured day and night to gain food for the
Divine Infant, for Mary, and for himself, and

* 'Solum in terris magni concilii coadjutorem fide-
lissimum' (*Homil.* II., *Sup. Missus est*).

his whole life was one service, or rather one perpetual sacrifice, which he offered to the Son of God made man, so that this great Saint did, himself alone, what the others did altogether.

VI.—*St. Joseph vicar of the three Persons of the most Holy Trinity.*

The prince of the Apostles is highly honoured for being the vicar of Jesus Christ upon earth, and it must be allowed that this dignity is great. But presently I shall show you, as I promised, that St. Joseph was the vicar on earth of all the three Persons of the adorable Trinity.

The Eternal Father appointed him His vicar. God, says the Abbot Rupert, delegated Joseph to discharge towards Jesus Christ all those offices which were incompatible with Divinity.* For this reason He communicated to him His own name of father; and as, in giving a name, God gives also the qualities belonging to that name, the heart of Joseph, as the Saints teach us, was so full of paternal

* 'Ad omnes labores, quos Deus ferre non poterat. Josephum pignorat' (Rupert.).

71

affection towards Jesus, that no one but God
and himself could express it. What greatness
to have with the Incarnate Word a relation of
paternity, similar, in a manner, to that of the
Eternal Father with the Uncreated Word! O
Father and father! O ineffable communication! O incomprehensible mystery! Can you,
O Joseph, think of it without trembling?
That He who said to God the Father, 'My
Father, give us this day our daily bread,'
should say also to you, 'My father, give us our
daily bread; for My Heavenly Father has entrusted this to your foresight and paternal
care'! St. Paul, to prove the divinity of Jesus
Christ, says: 'To which of the Angels hath He
said at any time, Thou art My Son?'* And
here, to show the dignity of Joseph, we must
say: 'To which of the Angels did the Incarnate
Word say at any time, Thou art My father?'
But what the Son of God never said to any
Angel, He said to a man, to Joseph, in whom
He recognised the vicar upon earth of His
Heavenly Father.

The Eternal Word also made him His vicar

* 'Cui dixit aliquando angelorum: Filius meus es
tu?' (Heb. i. 5).

and delegate. Tell me, I pray you, who is the greatest in the house of Nazareth? Certainly Joseph only follows after Jesus and Mary; and yet it is Joseph who commands them both. Jesus, during His infancy and hidden life, desires that Joseph should speak for Him, that he should act for Him, and for His Mother; that He and His Virgin Mother should remain hid, and that Joseph alone should appear.

The Holy Spirit, Who, in the Canticles, gives to the Immaculate Virgin the name of Spouse, has also constituted Joseph His vicar, since He chose him, above all men, to be the veritable spouse and protector of Our Lady.

My God! how unlimited is the confidence placed by the three Divine Persons in this holy man! The Father gives him His Son: the Son gives Himself in person to him; the Holy Spirit confides to him His spouse. The Father gives to him the entire charge of Jesus, constituting him the master of His only Son; the Son abandons Himself completely to his direction, doing nothing but in obedience to him; the Holy Spirit establishes him as angel guardian to Mary, and as head of the family of God. So that, while God governs all men, and the whole world, one man, upon earth, governs the Incarnate God and His most holy Mother, and does so by the express command of the Father, the Son, and the Holy Ghost.

Since, then, it has pleased the Most High, in His goodness, so marvellously to exalt this most blessed of Patriarchs, what honour should not be paid to him by heaven and earth, what love should not inflame our hearts for him! Should not our indifference and insensibility cover us with confusion? Great Saint, we most humbly beseech you in our own name, and that of all men, to pardon us; and, prostrate at your feet, from the bottom of our hearts, we desire to make reparation.

CHAPTER VIII.

THE ADMIRABLE AND INCOMPARABLE VIRTUES OF THIS HOLY PATRIARCH.

THE extraordinary graces with which it pleases God to enrich some of His servants are always infinitely precious ; but it is not in our own power to obtain them, and it would be temerity on our part to desire them, since they depend only on the pure liberality of One, Who gives them to whom He pleases, when He pleases, and as He pleases. Hitherto we have considered and admired the magnificence of the Almighty, with regard to St. Joseph, whom He crowned with incommunicable graces, or at least, graces so special, that they were communicated to no other than himself. But in this admirable Saint there are also actions and virtues which may be imitated. The eminent favours, of which we have spoken are glorious for him; the virtues, of which we shall now treat, have more utility for ourselves. The first excite in us the desire to pay him the homage due to him; the second give us the hope that, by imitating him, we may partake, in some small degree, of his glory; which is for us of the greatest importance.

I.—*His faith.*

The first virtue of St. Joseph is a faith so firm, that no trial, however rude, could shake it. St. John Chrysostom explains this, when he compares the seemingly contradictory words of the Angel at two different times. 'Fear not,' said the celestial messenger to Joseph, 'to take unto thee Mary thy wife, for that which is conceived in her is of the Holy Ghost. And she shall bring forth a son, and thou shalt call His name Jesus, for He shall save His people from their sins.' What could be more encouraging than such a promise! And yet, a short time after, the same messenger of God returns, and says to him: 'Take the Child and His Mother, and fly into Egypt; and be there until I shall tell thee; for it will come to pass that Herod will seek the Child to destroy Him.' 'Divine Archangel,' might Joseph have replied, 'your words contradict each other; how shall He save others, Who is incapable of saving Himself?' But no, he answered nothing, but rather chose to believe that the word of God would be accomplished in its proper time, and meanwhile executed without delay the orders he had received. How admirable was his faith when he believed, without a doubt, that his spouse was at once Virgin and Mother; when he believed, unhesitatingly, that the little Child, Whom he saw weeping and trembling on the straw, in a stable exposed to every wind, was indeed the God of heaven and of earth!

II.—*His purity.*

The purity of Joseph was quite angelical; or, according to St. Bernard, more than angelical, inasmuch as this virtue is more meritorious in men than in Angels. The holy virtue of virginity was so tenderly beloved by him, that had it been necessary to lose it, in becoming the spouse of the Virgin Mary, he would probably have chosen the virtue of the Angels, rather than the Queen of

Angels; while she also would have preferred to be a virgin without Divine maternity, rather than Mother of Gòd without virginity. Gerson has a very high idea of the excellence of St. Joseph's purity. He believes that he was sanctified in his mother's womb, and delivered from the source of concupiscence which singes and devastates human nature.* To me this opinion seems most probable. For if Jeremias was purified before his birth, who was only to be the prophet announcing the holy Word of God, how much more pressing were the reasons for granting the same favour to the spouse of Mary, the reputed father of the Messias, a man in constant communication with the Angels who came to confer with him about the order of the Incarnation, who, in a word, was one of the two flowers, the two lilies, between which the Word made flesh should take His delight!

* Gerson, *Serm. de Nativ. gloriosa V.M. et de commendatione virginei ejus Sponsi Joseph. Considerat.* ii. et iii.

III.—*His fidelity.*

The first quality required in one to whom treasures are entrusted is fidelity. Now, to Joseph the Almighty confided three precious deposits : the Mother of God, the Son of God, and the secret of God. St. Bernard admirably expresses it in these words : 'St. Joseph was chosen among all men, to be the protector and guardian of the Virgin Mother of God ; the defender and foster-father of the Infant-God, and the only co-operator upon earth, the one confidant of the secret of God in the work of the redemption of mankind.' What perfect fidelity was necessary to preserve with suitable care those three ineffable treasures !

IV.—*His humility.*

Origen, St. Bernard, and several other Fathers,* are overcome in contemplating the humility of this holy Patriarch. They believe that when he proposed to separate himself from Our Lady, it was because he considered himself unworthy to dwell under the same

* Origen., *Homil.* I., *in diversos Evangelistas.* — Bernard., *Homil.* II., *Super Missus est.*

roof with the Mother of God and Queen of Angels. 'Depart from me,' said St. Peter to Jesus Christ, 'for I am a sinful man'; in the same way Joseph, penetrated by a sense of his lowliness, said to himself: 'How unworthy I am to converse with this chosen Virgin, whom the Holy Spirit has filled with grace, and adorned with so many virtues!' Afterwards, when he saw the Infant God submit Himself in all things to his direction and orders, he felt that he could not descend low enough into the abyss of humility, and said to himself the words written later by St. Bernard: 'How shall a man not be humble in the presence of an humble God?'

V.—*His conformity to the Will of God.*

Our Lady revealed to St. Bridget, that her chaste spouse had constantly in his mouth these words: 'Heaven grant that I may live so as to accomplish the Will of my God!'* In the midst of his daily labours, this

---

* 'Totum desiderium suum fuit obedire voluntati Dei . . . Continue dicebat: Utinam vivam, et videam adimpletam voluntatem Dei' (S. Brigitt., Revelat., lib. 6, c. lix.).

sweet aspiration, this simple expression of entire conformity to the Divine Will, often escaped from his mouth and heart. He gave striking examples of this virtue, as well at the time of the sudden flight into Egypt, as in many other very painful circumstances. Then he adored the judgments of God in profound silence, submitting his will without any reserve to the orders of Divine Majesty. When he sought in vain among the inns of Bethlehem, for a place wherein to shelter his spouse and the Child she was about to bring into the world, not one complaint issued from his lips, and he felt quite content in the poor stable.

VI.—*His obedience.*

This virtue, the mother and guardian of all other virtues, has much in common with the preceding one. It was carried to such perfection by our glorious Saint, that St. John Chrysostom cannot sufficiently admire him for it. Never did he expostulate, when receiving a command from God; never did he excuse himself; never did he delay for one moment the execution. He is ordered to espouse the Virgin Mary; at once he agrees. Afterwards he is inspired to make the vow of chastity, which in that age was a thing unheard of, almost held as a disgrace; he obeys at once. He perceives that this Virgin more pure than the sun, is about to become a mother; a thousand thoughts pass through his mind: but when the Angel orders him not to quit her, he submits at once without uttering a word. After the departure of the three kings, he is told to fly to a distant country where he knows no one, where the demon is adored, where he will perhaps have to remain for years. How many objections would have presented themselves to a less submissive spirit! but either none of them presented themselves to the mind of Joseph, or he rejected them all; for the truly obedient man has hands for the work, and feet for motion: but he has no tongue wherewith to oppose the decrees of God and of obedience.

VII.—*His patience.*

His patience was admirable, and yet easy to imitate, for it consisted in bearing with resignation, and in silence, the trials which each day brought upon him. He was wont to consider all the events of life as the expression of the Divine Will, and therefore he adored from the bottom of his heart the eternal dispositions of Providence. He was ever willing to suffer without any sensible consolation, and esteemed himself happy in thus suffering. Consider how the Holy Family was banished into Egypt, reduced to poverty, persecuted and abandoned by the whole world. How great were the anxieties of Joseph for the safety of the Child and of the Mother! how great his labour for their support, while Heaven appeared to allow men to work their will, or even seemed to favour the enemies of Jesus! Amidst all these trials, Joseph suffered with invincible courage, and without uttering a word; or, if he did say anything, it was : ' My God, may I always live so as to accomplish Thy Will !'

VIII.—*His charity.*

His charity was most ardent, and his heart was burning with love for the amiable Divine Child, Whom he recognised to be the Son of the Eternal Father and of his most chaste spouse, the Desired of all nations, and the Saviour of the human race. When on the day of the presentation in the Temple, he had to redeem his firstborn, how gladly would he have given, instead of the two doves, his heart, his life, heaven and earth a thousand times over! How tender was his most pure love for that incomparable Virgin to whom he had been given as spouse! He knew that she was the well-beloved daughter of the Eternal Father, the well-beloved Mother of the Son of God, the well-beloved spouse of the Holy Ghost. He knew that this holiest and greatest of women respected him as her lord and master, loved him as the guardian of her virginal purity, and as, after God, the support of her own life and that of her Divine Son. You may imagine what ardent charity was burning in St. Joseph's soul. The God of his fathers, the God of Abraham, of Isaac, and of Jacob, had chosen his humble dwelling wherein to work the most astonishing of all miracles; He had confided to him, as to a good and faithful servant, His most intimate secrets! How could his heart escape being consumed, while constantly witnessing these marks of God's charity towards him, and ever abiding in the society of those two great teachers of divine love, Jesus and Mary!

IX.—*His modesty and love of silence.*

Most edifying and delightful is the modesty and silence of the holy Patriarch Joseph. A man so great, the lord and spouse of the Queen of the universe, the supposed father of the Messias, and yet so retiring that he never appears unless strictly obliged to do so; that he never utters a word unless it be for the service or defence of Jesus and Mary; that in his heart he esteems himself the lowest of men, a worm of the earth—is not this most strange and, to a carnal mind, altogether incomprehensible? At the birth of the Infant God the shepherds hasten in crowds to adore Him in the crib. Afterwards, the kings arrive from the East to prostrate themselves at His feet, and offer Him presents. On different occasions the Angels appear to Mary and to Joseph, conversing familiarly with them. On the day of purification Simeon and Anna say marvellous things of the Divine Child, and, in their praises, forget neither the Virgin Mother nor the blessed man who is regarded as the father of Jesus. Do you believe that the honours attached to such rare privileges excite in his heart the least sentiment of self-complacency ? Observe but his conduct. If anything must be said, he lets his dearest consort speak, leaving all the honour to her, withdrawing himself from the attention of men. He speaks with Jesus and with Mary, but that only rarely, and in the retirement of their household ; beyond that, he has no other eloquence but that of silence and modesty.

Consider the manner in which he governed the Holy Family. Assuredly, there never was a man at the head of such an empire, since he had for his subjects the King of kings, and the Queen of heaven and earth. But how could he, who was so modest, command Jesus and Mary ; he who esteemed himself unworthy to be under their feet, or to look them in the face ? He commanded by requesting ; he governed by beseeching, or rather, he himself did all, for I am convinced that he much preferred doing to commanding. But, on the other side, we may also suppose that Jesus and Mary, the Master and the Mistress of humility, use gentle violence to overcome the modesty of Joseph, and constrain him to submit to the order of God the Father, Who had established him as His representative upon earth. O empire, like to none other! All three are superiors, all three are inferiors, all three masters, all three subjects. No one wishes to command, each one perfectly fulfils what he has got to do, while the most entire subordination is observed, and the most admirable obedience is practised.

X.—*His devotion.*

The devotion of St. Joseph was perfect in every point, since he possessed all its characteristics in an eminent degree. The masters of spiritual life esteem highly devotion to the presence of God, and they regard it, with reason, as one of the most efficacious means of attaining to perfection; according to the words of God to His servant Abraham: 'Walk before Me, and be perfect.'* But who ever practised this holy exercise better than St. Joseph, who had the Lord Jesus and His holy Mother constantly before his eyes? To others God is only present by faith; to Joseph He was present both corporeally and spiritually, without interruption, and without distraction of any kind.

When St. Peter saw his Divine Master in the splendour of His glory on Mount Thabor he cried: 'Lord, it is good for us to be here; if Thou wilt, let us make here three tabernacles: one for Thee, and one for Moses, and one for Elias,' and let us never leave this happy abode. Now, the entire life of St. Joseph was like a day of transfiguration, without any evening. Every day he contemplated the divine Face of the Infant Jesus; he beheld the white cloud—I mean his holy spouse, in which the Sun of Justice had concealed Him-

---

* 'Ego Deus omnipotens; ambula coram me, et esto perfectus' (Gen. **xvii.** 1).

self during nine months; He lived under the same roof with them. O how good it was for him to abide in that house more delightful than the terrestrial paradise, more holy than the Holy of Holies!

Let us pass to some other comparison. The holy Church, our Mother, desiring from time to time to rekindle the devotion of her children by her pious solemnities, has established the forty hours exposition of the Blessed Sacrament. But was not the whole life of Joseph a continuation of these forty hours, an uninterrupted vision of Jesus Christ, a perpetual jubilee, a continual transport, a daily colloquy with God? and mark here the special character of Joseph's devotion. He saw in Jesus Christ at once God and man, a father and a son; he addressed Him at the same time with the respect of a son, and the authority of a father. We understand well the kind of devotion which begs and implores, for it is the devotion of all the Saints; but the devotion which supplicates in commanding is known alone to St. Joseph and his most holy spouse; it belongs to them exclusively and to no other. Yes, even in addressing his prayer to the Incarnate Word, Joseph uses the paternal authority given him by God, and the Son of God Himself desires that it should be so; He chooses to obey him as a son, and to do all that he commands.

We will conclude this subject with pointing out some particular features in the devotion of the glorious St. Joseph.

Firstly. His contemplation was at once very sublime and very profound. Who can imagine what fervour, both sweet and burning, martyrized his soul; what unutterable joys the presence of those two Divine objects, Jesus and Mary, often produced in him? From them he learned the secrets of that sublime devotion which transforms the life of man into intimate intercourse with God.

Secondly. That state of the soul which is called ecstasy was habitual with him. For, having at his disposal the two sources of devotion—I mean the Saviour and His most sweet Mother—he felt 'inebriated with the plenty of God's house, and was made to drink of the torrent of His pleasure.'*

Thirdly. Often there escaped from his

* Psa. xxxv. 9.

breast sighs, intermingled with tender and heart-felt words, or ejaculatory prayers which he launched, with force, like fiery darts into the Heart of God, knowing well that 'the kingdom of heaven suffereth violence, and the violent bear it away.'*

Fourthly. It was easy for him to raise his soul to God. Indeed, what others have got to seek in heaven, he had in his own house, and close at hand. But when he raised his eyes from the vision of the humanity of the Word Incarnate up to its Divinity, O God, how must his heart have melted within him, and what transports must he have experienced! I am inclined to believe that the habitual sight of Jesus and Mary would have made his life one continual ecstasy, had not the effect, which these two Divine objects would naturally have produced on him, been moderated by a miraculous power.

Fifthly. The light which filled his mind, and the knowledge communicated to him by God of the most profound mysteries, are things which it is easy to believe but very difficult to understand. The royal prophet

* Matt. xi. 12.

says : 'With Thee is the fountain of life, and in Thy light we shall see light.'* What an abundance of knowledge did this holy Patriarch draw from the heart of the Word Uncreated and Incarnate, and into what depths was his soul plunged!

Sixthly. To come into contact with God fills the soul with happiness ; but who ever experienced this as Joseph did ? He conversed daily with Jesus and Mary, and his whole life was a continual intercourse with God. While St. Antony, kneeling beside St. Paul, the first hermit, mingled his prayers with his, his heart was as if on fire. Imagine, then, how the heart of Joseph was inflamed when he prayed, when he meditated, when he offered himself entirely to God the Father, in company with the Divine Infant Jesus, and with the Virgin his spouse.

Seventhly. Who can describe the divine communications, the visits of God into a heart of such perfect dispositions ? When the eyes of Jesus met those of Joseph, what an impression must have been made on his soul, and

* 'Quoniam apud te est fons vitæ ; et in lumine tuo videbimus lumen' (Psa. xxxv. 10).

what an abundance of heavenly graces must
have flowed into the breast of this man, who
was indeed more favoured than the Seraphim!

Eighthly. His soul was an abode of peace,
happiness, and heavenly delights. St. Francis
Xavier and St. Ephrem, when receiving divine
consolations, cried out that they could bear
no more and live: what must St. Joseph have
felt when he saw himself the object of the
love and tenderness of Jesus, of Mary, and of
the Angels of heaven! 'It is enough,' he re-
peated gently, 'it is enough!'

Ninthly. The highest summit of spiritual
life is the close union of an extremely pure
soul with God, Who is the essence of purity.
Could Jesus have found on earth a soul more
innocent than that of His foster-father, a soul
which He loved with more tender affection,
and of which He could say with more truth:
'I love them that love Me . . . and My delights
are to be with the children of men'?* Certainly not. No one, except the blessed Mother
of God, has ever equalled in devotion that
holy Patriarch St. Joseph.

* 'Ego diligentes me diligo . . . et deliciæ meæ esse
cum filiis hominum' (Prov. viii. 17, 31).

XI.—*All his other virtues.*

That the soul of St. Joseph was adorned with all virtues is a truth that we would loudly proclaim, even had it not been expressly affirmed by St. Bernardin of Siena. ' I believe,' says that great light of the Seraphic Order, 'that the spouse of Mary, and foster-father of Jesus, was endowed with virginity most pure, humility most profound, charity most ardent, contemplation most sublime, and most ardent zeal for the salvation of men, after the example of the most holy Virgin, to whom the Holy Spirit would not have given him as spouse, had he not been her faithful likeness.'* What renders St. Joseph still more dear to me, is that, as Gerson relates, the face of Jesus and his face resembled each other perfectly ; for grace, which often is pleased to imitate nature, had given the Infant Jesus features which made Him appear the real son

* ' Credo istum virum sanctum Joseph, fuisse mundissimum in virginitate, profundissimum in humilitate, ardentissimum in Dei amore et charitate, altissimum in contemplatione, sollicitissimum pro hominum salute, ad similitudinem illius Virginis sponsæ suæ ' (*Serm. de S. Joseph*, art. 2, c. i.).

of Joseph.* But oh! my God, how much closer
was the resemblance between his heart and
the Heart of Jesus, since in the one as in
the other was to be found the union of all
virtues! Only in heaven, great Saint, shall
we see your merits in all their splendour; for
as long as you were on earth, your extreme
humility kept all your treasures hidden in
your heart.

XII.—*The uninterrupted growth of all virtues.*

Although we know but very imperfectly the
ineffable virtues of Joseph, we can be very
sure that, as a good and faithful servant, he
was careful to make fruitful the talent confided to him by the Lord. ' The path of the
just,' says the Wise Man, ' as a shining light
goeth forwards and increaseth even to perfect
day.'† Even the name of Joseph expresses this
continual progress, since it signifies ' augmen-
tation, increase.'

* ' Facies Jesu erat similis faciei Joseph ; similem
autem non caro, sed gratia fecit, gratia enim sæpe
naturæ consona vult fieri.'
† ' Justorum autem semita quasi lux splendens pro-
cedit, et crescit usque ad perfectam diem' (Prov. iv. 18).

One must have got but a poor idea of the
greatness of our Saint, were he to discourse
at greater length upon such an incontest-
able truth? Indeed, if it be true, as Gerson
believes, that St. Joseph was sanctified in the
womb of his mother; if it be true that the fire
of concupiscence, which inclines the heart of
man to evil, was extinguished or repressed in
this privileged man; if it be true that from his
birth he was endowed with the most special
graces of Heaven; how could he fail to
advance daily in the path of perfection?* Add
the impression which the sweet and powerful
examples of Jesus and of Mary must have
made on his soul. The Child, as St. Luke
tells us, advanced daily in wisdom and age,
and grace with God and men. As for the
most holy Virgin, the Saints tell us that such
was the impression her presence produced,
that people could not look at her without

* 'Maria sicut fuerat in utero sanctificata prius-
quam nasceretur, ita de Joseph, virginali viro suo, pia
credulitate credi potest quamvis non omnino similiter'
(*Serm. de Nativ. B.V.*, Considerat. ii.). 'Maria sicut
habuit repressionem fomitis originalis, ne in vitiosam
excandesceret concupiscentiam; ita de Joseph, sponso
suo intelligi pie potest, præsertim dum matrimonialiter
eidem conjunctus est' (Considerat. iii.).

becoming more virtuous.* How then could Joseph, unceasingly dwelling in the presence of Jesus and Mary, have been one single moment without growing in sanctity ?

It was for the great Gerson a subject of regret, and almost of temptation, that he had not been able to hear the ordinary conversations of St. Joseph with Our Lady, or with the Child Jesus, or with both together.† He does not doubt that St. Joseph inquired from the Blessed Virgin the true meaning of the 'Magnificat,' of the 'Benedictus' of Zacharias, and of the 'Nunc dimittis' of Simeon ; that he asked her about all that the Angel had said to her of the Child, and about all those other things which she kept so carefully in her heart. Also his holy spouse, being filled with the light of the Holy Spirit, discovered to him the most sublime mysteries, and all the secrets of the Incarnation. If Elizabeth was filled with prophetic spirit at the first word she heard from the mouth of Mary ;

* 'Eam (concupiscentiam) potius extinguebat ille divinus aspectus, quasi frigidus quidam ex oculis ros virgineus spiraret vel efflueret a mente sua castissima ' (Gerson, *Serm. citato*).

† 'Quis det interfuisse collocutionibus hujusmodi ?' (*Serm. citato*).

if it caused St. John the Baptist to leap in the womb of his mother; if the holy old man Simeon desired to die after having seen Him Who was the salvation of Jacob, and the light of the Gentiles; if Anne the prophetess was so transported as to speak of the Infant God to all who looked for the redemption of Israel; what must have been the condition of St. Joseph's heart, who, during so many years, spoke every day so familiarly with his dear spouse, and her Son Jesus Christ, and who listened to the replies they so willingly gave to all his questions! No one can imagine how sublime was his knowledge of all the mysteries of faith, and the ineffable greatness of God; for he learned all, either from the Archangels who often spoke to him, or from Our Lady who conferred with him every day, or from Jesus Who was his chief teacher.

Gerson is carried even farther by his devotion to St. Joseph. 'Ah!' he exclaims, 'why can I not hear the voice of Our Lady, when, to rejoice her Divine Son, she sang to Him the songs of Sion, and the hymns of Paradise?'*

---

* ' Quis det hymnum de canticis Sion ex Maria suaviter audivisse in terra aliena ?' (*Serm. cit.*, Considerat. iii.).

Must not St. Joseph whenever he listened
to this, more than seraphic, voice, have been
moved even to tears ? We know only one
canticle of the Blessed Virgin, the 'Magnificat ;' but how often may the Holy Spirit have
inspired her with others as beautiful, even more
beautiful, since they were composed for the
Incarnate Word ! St. Francis of Assisi once
heard an Angel sing, and he thought he
must have died of joy ; how is it that Joseph
did not die each time that he heard the
Queen of Angels either sing, or discourse with
her Blessed Son, and that he listened to the
divine replies of this Oracle of heaven and of
earth ?

From songs, Gerson passes to tears. He sup-
poses, according to the general opinion, that
St Joseph died before the time of the Passion,
for otherwise the Saviour would not on the
Cross have recommended His Mother to St.
John. He then continues: 'It is my belief
that when St. Joseph was dying, he was
assisted by Jesus and Mary, and that, since
virtue makes natural affection more perfect,
Jesus wept for His foster-father and served
him in his last illness, consoling and strength-

ening him for the final passage. I believe
that his holy spouse mingled her tears with
those of her Son, weeping with tenderness for
her well-beloved spouse, and thanking him
affectionately for all the services he had
rendered her.'* And why should not Jesus
have shed tears at the death of Joseph His
father, as he afterwards shed them at the
death of Lazarus His friend ? But who can
describe to us the feelings of the holy Patriarch, when he saw himself the object
of such tears ? Who can make us understand the divine consolations with which
Jesus inundated his soul, and the words
of sweetness addressed to him by the most
holy Mother of God, his spouse ? Never did
man repeat with more truth those touching
words : 'Lord, into Thy hands I commend my
spirit,' since with humble confidence he
committed his into the hands of the Son of
God Himself, Who had chosen him to be His
guardian and His father. Could there be a
death more holy, or in more holy company ?

* 'Christus adest cum matre pia,' etc. (Gerson,
Josephina, Distinct. xii.).

CHAPTER IX.

IS IT POSSIBLE TO PRAISE OUR LADY AND ST.
JOSEPH IN A MANNER WORTHY OF THEM?
CONTEST BETWEEN THE ABBOT TRITHEMIUS ON
THE ONE SIDE, AND ST. BERNARD AND OTHER
SAINTS ON THE OTHER.

THE celebrated and venerable Abbot Trithemius* of the order of St. Benedict, one of
the ornaments of his age, and of the lights of
Germany, was an ardent lover of Our Lady.
The proof whereof you may find in his books
in which he extols the Mother of God in the
very highest terms, and places her on the
most elevated pinnacle. Nay, he even seems
to defy all others to say anything better in
her praise. But here, as it were, St. Bernard
takes up the challenge. Let the reader be

---

* Author of the *Traité des illustres Ecrivains ecclé-
siastiques*, and of several other pious and learned works.
He died in 1516, at the age of fifty-four.

judge which of the two is more eloquent in her praise. But, at the same time let him remember that, to whichever side the balance inclines, the cause of Mary must always gain, and that, whatever is said in her praise, must also turn to the glory of her spouse.

1. Trithemius begins by borrowing the words of a French poet,* and says : 'Could you transform into tongues all the grains of sea-sand, all the floods of the ocean, the drops of rain, the flakes of snow, the flowers of the fields, the leaves of the forest, and the stars of the firmament, could you employ the tongues of all the animals that are upon the earth, and of all the birds which fly in the air, you would still be unable to celebrate the Mother of God, in a manner worthy of her.' Is it possible to say more ?

' Yes,' replies St. Bernard, 'one must add : If all the Angels wished to explain to us the marvels operated by God in Mary, in spite of all their knowledge and of all the love which

---

* Peter Comestor, a native of Troyes, canon of that town, and chancellor of the Church of Paris in the twelfth century.—Joan. Trithem. *de Miraculis Beatiss. Mariæ semper Virginis in Ecclesia nova prope Dittelbach factis*, lib. 1, c. x.

animates them for their Queen, they never would succeed, for none other than the Author of this divine masterpiece is capable of praising it according to its deserts.'

Let us make an application of this to St. Joseph. Our Lady revealed to St. Bridget that all that has been said in her praise may be generally and proportionately applied to her spouse. She is the handmaid of the Lord; Joseph is His good and faithful servant, and so with the rest. 'It would be a small thing for Mary,' says St. Augustine, 'to have been Mother of God according to the flesh, had she not first been so according to the spirit, by her faith, her obedience, and her love.' But was not St. Joseph father of Jesus Christ according to the spirit, by the practice of all virtues? And as this spiritual paternity is very agreeable to God, and St. Joseph possessed it in the most sublime manner, it follows, from the passages quoted above, that no tongue can give us an idea of the excellence of this great Patriarch.

2. 'The Virgin Mary,' continues Abbot Trithemius, 'whom God preserved from all stain, even of original sin, is the fountain of

salvation, the fulness of grace, the reparation of mankind.' Can anything be added to these praises?

'Yes,' reply St. Bernard and St. Bonaventure, 'she is not merely a fountain, she is an ocean; she is not merely full of grace, but full of God Himself, and of all the plenitude of the Most Holy Trinity.' As St. Peter Damian says, the plenitude of Divinity has descended into her; and St. Chrysostom adds : ' You speak to us of a brook, of a rivulet of water, while we speak to you of an abyss which has neither bottom nor shore.'

But who is the master of this fountain, the owner of this ocean? Who has the keys of this abyss, from which he may draw when he will and what he will? Is it not Joseph, the general administrator and representative of the Holy Spirit upon earth? Behold, how whatever is said to the praise of Mary, likewise redounds to the glory of Joseph.

3. 'I maintain,' continues the learned Abbot, 'that Mary is the pearl of virginity, the ark of eternal salvation, a cloud filled with divine abundance, a treasure of all purity.' Can you, I pray, find more glorious titles than these?

Still the other Saints go beyond all that and say: 'The most excellent Virgin is not merely an ark, but the paradise of the second Adam; she is not a cloud, but a golden firmament, more vast than the immensity of the universe; she is not merely a treasure for herself, but an inexhaustible source of spiritual riches for all who place themselves under her protection, and implore with filial confidence the help of her holy prayers.'

Now, St. Joseph is a pearl resembling in all points that other pearl. It is he who has the golden key of that ark; who distributes all the riches and all the treasures it contains; who is the first to participate in all these glories. In a word, as there is nothing which so resembles a diamond as another diamond from the same mine, so there is no other so resembling the Mother of Jesus as that happy man who is called by Jesus His father. Truly, we cannot praise the Mother of Christ, without allowing the same praises to His foster-father.

4. Mary is the house of gold, in which Divinity makes His abode; she is the foundation of all perfection, the mirror of holy

simplicity, in which Angels may contemplate and admire the incomparable excellence of their sovereign princess. These are the words of Trithemius.

'Alas!' reply St. Bernard and St. Peter Damian, 'why be so niggardly in praising the Queen of the universe, the Mother of the Creator and Redeemer of the world? You say she is the golden house of Divinity; say rather that her heart, her soul, her whole being is transformed into pure love of God, and that, since she carried God in her breast, everything in her is, so to speak, deified. She is not merely the mirror of the Angels, but the mirror of God Himself, Who has made her so beautiful that He cannot look on her without exclaiming: "How beautiful are thy steps, O daughter of the Prince! and thy walk, how full of grace!" If what is the least great in this Queen, I mean her walk and deportment, already transports the heart of the spouse, what must be her face, her heart, her soul, and her entire person, which partakes the charms of all that is beautiful in the world, and, indeed, surpasses it, as light chases away darkness!'

But, as God and His Angels take their complacency in Mary, thus Mary turns to Joseph and acknowledges him to be the mirror of virginal purity, and the masterpiece that proceeded from the hands of the Most High.

5. Once more Trithemius returns to praising the Mother of God. 'Mary,' he says, 'is the aurora of eternal happiness, the splendour of divine knowledge, the palace of clemency and of all heavenly sweetness.'

And yet the other Saints, as it were, consider these to be but poor praises in comparison of what Our Lady deserves. You call her the dawn of day, but why not affirm with St. Bernard, that she is a living ray of Divinity, and more resplendent than the sun ? She is not merely the palace, but the mother of clemency and mercy. Who then is the man who, above all the world, praises most eloquently the Queen of Paradise ? It is he who ingenuously confesses that nothing he can say can equal the extent of her almost boundless perfections.

Consider now, that to St. Joseph belongs this spouse, with all that she possesses in the world. God spared nothing in enriching her who was to be His Mother; and when He had overwhelmed her with His favours, He gave her to this fortunate man, who was so little in his own eyes, and so great in the eyes of the Lord.

6. Trithemius, as it were, makes yet another attempt to carry off the palm in the praises of Mary. He states eight reasons, which we refrain from quoting, to show that a great number of temples should be erected all over the earth, in which all men might be invited to honour in a worthy manner the most holy Mother of God, and her blessed spouse. Though the mouth and heart of one man, or even of many together be incapable of honouring them sufficiently, let all men, without exception, he says, unite in singing their praises.

'No,' reply the other side, 'this would not be enough. Let the whole universe be but one temple: its vault, the sky; its lights, the stars; its incense, the perfume of the flowers; its music, the songs of birds; its ornaments, all the riches of nature; its ministers, all mankind. All hearts of men and of Angels should be so many temples dedicated to the honour of Jesus, of His sweet Mother, and of the Patriarch St. Joseph. There should be gathered the palms of the martyrs, the laurels of the Apostles, the lilies and roses of the virgins, all the sanctity of Paradise to form one chapel of light, in which to erect three altars, the first for Jesus, the second for Mary, and the third for Joseph.'

But let us raise our thoughts still higher: let us say that three temples should be prepared for the Virgin Mary: the first, in the Heart of the Eternal Father; the second, in the Heart of the Uncreated Word; the third, in the Heart of the Holy Ghost; and then, even, must St. Joseph be placed beside her. For if St. Elzear was justified in writing to his spouse, St. Delphine, that the abode in which she could always find him was the Heart of Jesus Christ, why should not we be allowed to say that the Queen of the Seraphim should dwell in the Heart of the three Divine Persons? There it is the Queen of the world must abide, not in temples made of dust. There all men and all Angels must contemplate her, so as to exalt as much as they are capable of doing, the glory of this chosen

Virgin, and of her incomparable spouse; and
when they have done so let them even confess
that it belongs to God alone to praise worthily
these chief marvels of His almightiness and
mercy.*

* It is certain that though Abbot Trithemius praises
the Mother of God in a most beautiful and varied
manner, he is far from flattering himself that he has
done so as much as it is possible to do. If our author
seems to insinuate the contrary, we must say that he
has made use of an innocent fiction in order to give
more life and interest to his subject.—(*Note of the
Editor.*) Also, since Abbot Trithemius lived so long
after the Saints with whom he is supposed to have had
a contest, it is evident that Father Binet it is who has
put into that form quotations from their different
works.

CHAPTER X.

THE GLORY OF ST. JOSEPH.

THE most holy Virgin, as related above, revealed to St. Bridget, that St. Joseph frequently made use of these beautiful words: 'Heaven grant that I may live so as to accomplish the will of my God!' And she added: 'Therefore it is that the glory of Joseph is now so great.'* These words at first sight are plain enough. But to understand them fully, we ought to remember how moderate, in her assertions, Our Lady was. Had she wished to point out an object most sublime, she would simply have said: 'It is great.' Thus when Elizabeth said to her, 'Blessed art thou that hast believed, because those things shall be accomplished that were spoken to thee by the Lord,' her reply was,

* 'Ideo nunc gloria sua magna est' (Revelat., lib. 6, c. lix.).

'The Lord hath done great things to me,' which means things quite ineffable. In the same way, when she says, 'The glory of my spouse is great,' we must understand that it surpasses all that can be imagined in this world.

Divine glory, according to St. Bernardin of Siena, plunges this great Patriarch into the infinite ocean of Divinity, absorbs him as in a bottomless abyss. His heart is not vast enough to receive all the glory prepared for him by God: hence, it is not God Who enters into him, but he it is that enters into, and loses himself in the Heart of God.* When on earth, Joseph received the Incarnate Word into his house, he pressed Him to his breast, and, had it been possible, would have wished to make Him enter into his heart. Is it not reasonable that now the same Word, receiving him into the house of His glory, should also press him to His Heart, and make him enter so profoundly into His Divinity, as, in a manner, to identify Himself with him ? Formerly, the looks, the caresses, even the breath of the Infant God† had been the unutterable

---

* S. Bernardin., *Serm. de S. Joseph*, art. 2, c. ii.

† 'Cum filiali aspectu, afflatu atque amplexu' (*Serm. de S. Joseph*, art. 2, c. ii.).

delight of His adopted father : but now God shows the same, His glorious divine countenance, and rewards him with the embrace of His infinite perfection.

Theologians teach that the amount of grace acquired in this life is the measure of the glory to be received in heaven. If this be true, which we cannot doubt, we may be sure that St. Joseph's place in the heavenly Jerusalem is an extremely high one. Let us hear what the learned Chancellor of Paris says on this point. In his sermon on the Nativity of the Blessed Virgin, which he preached before the Fathers of the Council of Constance, he makes two assertions, the first of which is: 'I cannot tell you, my Fathers, which is the most admirable, the humility of Mary, or the sublimity of Joseph.'* Now the humility of Our Lady being, so to speak, infinite, what must we think of the equally surprising greatness of her holy spouse ? Verily, if Jesus Christ still calls Joseph His father, and if the Blessed Virgin still calls him her lord, how

---

* 'Nescio sane, Patres orthodoxi, hic quid amplius habeat mirabilius, vel humilitas in Maria, vel in Joseph sublimitas' (*Serm. de Nativitate B.M.V.*, Considerat. iv.).

ineffable is his glory! If he, of all men, holds still a claim to these titles in the presence of all Angels and Saints, how exalted must be his station amongst them!

The second proposition of Gerson is as follows: 'Who will give me words to explain worthily the ineffable mystery of this admirable Trinity, Jesus, Mary, Joseph?'* For those three persons, are a true and living image of the adorable Trinity, where there is one Father, one Son, and one Spirit, Who is the bond, the love, and the gift of both. Here also we find a father, a son, and the immaculate heart of a Virgin, who is the love of both, and who forms a very close bond, uniting father to son, and son to father, mother to son, son to mother, husband to wife, and wife to husband. A bond so identifying, that these three hearts seem to be no longer three, but one and the same heart.

From this sublime doctrine the learned chancellor draws the following conclusion:

* 'Cuperem mihi verba suppeterent ad explicandum tam altum et absconditum a sæculis mysterium, tam admirandam venerandamque Trinitatem Jesu, Mariæ et Joseph' (*Ibid.*).

'Where I am,' says our Lord Jesus, 'there also shall My minister be.' Since, then, Joseph was, with Our Lady, the nearest to Him upon earth, why should he not be, after Mary, the nearest to Jesus in heaven?* Great God! can anything more be said in his praise? Alas! how little devotion, how little love is ours for a man endowed with so many graces, and crowned with such glory!

It is here the place to remember an opinion of several learned authors, which we have already mentioned before. They think that St. Joseph is in heaven body as well as soul, having followed Our Saviour thither on Ascension Day. 'It is a pious belief,' say St. Bernardin of Siena and Suarez,† 'that St. Joseph and Our Lady are, body and soul, with Jesus Christ in the delightful life of glory, as they were together in the laborious life of exile.' This opinion is confirmed by the

---

* 'Profecto si non mentiebatur Jesus, qui ait: "Ubi sum ego, illic et minister meus erit" (Joan. xii. 26): ille proximior videtur collocandus in cœlis, qui in ministerio fuit vicinior, obsequentior, atque fidelior post Mariam inventus in terris' (Gerson, *loco citato*).

† S. Bernardin., *Serm. de S. Joseph.* art. 3.—Suarez, *De Incarnat.*, p. 2, disp. 8, sect. 2.

doctrine of those theologians who consider the order of grace in Our Lady and St. Joseph to be a hierarchy apart, destined for the immediate service of the divine person of the Messias. Now, if thus pre-eminence is given to them among all other Saints of the Church militant, St. Bernardin believes that they must likewise occupy the highest rank in the Church triumphant; and that there, above all Saints and Angels, Jesus, Mary, and Joseph form a Trinity apart, enjoying a love, a glory, and a union so sublime and so intimate, that in this hierarchy there is only room for those three. You may safely conclude from this, that St. Joseph is the greatest Saint in heaven. The pious and learned Suarez does not hesitate to say : 'It is not an article of faith, but a well-founded pious belief, that St. Joseph surpasses all other Saints in grace and in glory, and that he is, in body and soul, the nearest to Jesus and Mary in heaven, as he was the nearest to them while on earth.'*

'Give, and it shall be given to you; good measure, and pressed down, and shaken to-

* Suarez, *De Incarnat.*. p. 2, disp. 8, sect. 2.

gether, and running over shall they give into
your bosom; for with the same measure that
you shall mete withal, it shall be measured
to you again.'* Let this rule be observed
with regard to St. Joseph. What, indeed, did
he not give to the Incarnate Word! He
gave Him his house to dwell in, his heart
as a place of sweet repose, his hands to
nourish Him by their labour. Now Jesus
Christ renders him abode for abode, heart
for heart, measure for measure in the
glory of heaven. All other Saints, even
the greatest in dignity and glory, are only
servants, and are treated as servants; while
Joseph is the legal father, the reputed father,
the foster-father of Jesus, and is therefore
treated as father. Glory does not change the
natural relations, but brings them to perfection. Wherefore this admirable Patriarch,
who constantly had the honour of commanding Jesus and Mary, and the happiness of
serving them all his life, with incomparable
love and fidelity, stands now highest in the
glory of heaven. Truly my spirit loses itself
in these ineffable heights, and the splendour

* Luke vi. 38.

of that incomparable glory dazzles me and
reduces me to silence. I can but ask the
pardon of this great and amiable Saint for
treating of his excellence in so unworthy a
manner.

When Joseph, after some months of virginal
marriage, desired, in his humility, to separate
himself from his holy spouse, it was necessary,
that Gabriel should again descend from heaven
and address these words to him: Joseph,
son of David, fear not; do not separate yourself from your spouse; it is the will of God
that you live in the same house with her,
since you are one in heart. If Joseph, seeing
his spouse so great and so elevated in heaven,
should now, in respectful awe, wish to
separate himself from her, it seems to me
God would send a Seraph to say to him: 'Fear
not, Joseph; nor think of separating yourself
either from Jesus or from Mary; the Eternal
Father desires that you remain near His Son,
because on earth you occupied His place
beside Him; the Son wills that you remain
near Him, because you were His foster-father;
the Holy Spirit commands you to remain near
Mary, because you were the guardian-angel

of His chaste spouse ; Mary demands that the
order of the three Divine Persons be respected,
because you are her spouse; and all the inhabitants of the heavenly court declare, with
one voice, that your place is beside Jesus and
Mary, and that those whom God united, during so many years, on earth, must not be
separated in heaven.' My heart rejoices, O
great Saint, to see you so closely and so in-
separably united to Jesus and Mary in glory.
Never shall I separate you from the Son, nor
from the Mother, in my devotions and prayers ;
and may I always be the humble and most
happy client of Jesus, of Mary, and of Joseph.

CHAPTER XI.

THE POWER OF ST. JOSEPH.

ONE cannot wonder that this great Patriarch should be so powerful, seeing that he commands the two authorities of heaven and earth, Jesus and Mary. The learned Gerson speaks of him as a protector, influential, powerful, almost all-powerful,* since he is the reputed father, the foster-father, and guardian of Jesus, and the spouse, the protector, and the guardian of Mary. What can be refused to the man who produces titles so valid and authentic as these ? Besides, whatever Jesus demands from His Heavenly Father, the Father wills; whatever Our Lady demands from her beloved Son, the Son wills; and whatever Joseph demands from his holy spouse, she wills. Does it not follow that as Mary is all-powerful

* 'Magne Joseph . . . imperiose patrone' (*Josephina*, sub finem).

through Jesus, Joseph is all-powerful through Mary? Oh, how good it is to have St. Joseph for advocate, since nothing in the world is impossible to him!

The other Saints supplicate Jesus and Mary, St. Joseph commands them; this bold idea of Origen has been adopted by several Doctors. St. Joseph speaks as a father; but a father does not petition his son, he commands him. The other Saints throw down their crowns at the feet of the Lamb, and pray as suppliants; St. Joseph supplicates as one commanding, or rather, the humility of this holy man is too great to permit him to command the Lord Jesus; but the goodness of Our Lord is so condescending, that He accepts the prayers of Joseph as paternal commands, and grants all he requests. Happy Patriarch! who alone of all men has relations so special, union so intimate with the Saviour of the world, and His most holy Mother! The Son of Mary owes obedience to you; your spouse owes you honour, you have the right to command them both; can you then fear to pray to them for your clients?

When two just men consent upon earth

concerning anything whatever that they
demand in the name of Jesus Christ, it shall
be granted to them by His Father in heaven.*
Here, indeed, is this promise of the Saviour
verified. When Mary and Joseph plead
together before the throne of their Divine
Son, in favour of one of their servants, is there
any grace which they cannot obtain? Great
God! give to me those two all-powerful
advocates; grant that they may always plead
my cause before Thine adorable Majesty, and
that I may ever render to them acceptable
service. Where is there to be found an object
more beloved by Thee and more worthy of our
love than those two noble hearts?

When I think on the history of Jacob return-
ing to the land of his fathers, my heart is
filled with hope. He and Rachel, holding their
son Joseph by the hand, advanced in confidence, and when they arrived before Esau,
they appeased the wrath of this fierce man.
Even so, I imagine that if Mary and Joseph,
holding Jesus by the hand, present themselves
before God the Father in my favour, His just
wrath must infallibly be calmed, the thunder-

* Matt. xviii. 19.

bolt will fall from His hands, and He will look on me with favour. So powerful is the intercession of Jesus, Mary, and Joseph, when they have taken in hand the cause of a poor sinner.

St. John, exiled to Patmos, where he wrote the Apocalypse, was one day rapt in spirit, and beheld ' a throne set in heaven, and upon the throne one sitting. And He that sat was to the sight like the jasper and the sardine stone ; and there was a rainbow round about the throne, in sight like unto an emerald.'* Some authors thus explain this vision. The throne is the most pure Virgin Mary; He Who sits upon the throne is Jesus Christ our Saviour ; the rainbow which surrounds Jesus and Mary are all the Saints, but more especially Joseph, to whom God confided the care of the Child and of His Mother. This iris, by which I mean our holy Patriarch, shines between two clouds of glory, and is adorned with all the beauties of Paradise, being the symbol of mercy, and the precious pledge of divine goodness. At the sight of this bow, God promises to pardon human nature, and to

* Apoc. iv. 2, 3.

forget His just resentment. Another explanation is, that Jesus, Mary, and Joseph are themselves the three principal colours of the bow of hope and salvation which surrounds the throne of the Most High. The red is the Blood of Jesus; the blue, the purity of Our Lady; the green, the sanctity of Joseph. These three heavenly colours have the virtue of arresting and appeasing the wrath of God the Father. 'I shall,' He says, 'see the bow, and shall remember My covenant with you, that there shall no more be waters of a flood to destroy all flesh. This shall be the sign of the covenant which I have established between Me and all flesh upon the earth.' Will you then, reader, have, if not perfect certainty, at least a well-founded hope of your salvation? Accept the promise of this heavenly rainbow, Jesus, Mary, Joseph; accept the influence of their holy inspirations, and the numberless graces with which they enrich their servants. Gerson recounts that those who, having lost any object, recommend themselves to St. Joseph, are sure to find it again.* He cites the example of a friend of his; but

---

* *Josephina*, sub finem.

I believe the friend is no other than himself. Alas! we have lost God by sin, and in losing God we have lost Paradise, we have lost all! Let us often say to our holy Protector those words of the Gospel: 'Sir, we would see Jesus.'* Sweet Joseph, we have lost Jesus Christ; will not you show Him to us, and give Him back to our souls? Mary and Joseph, we have lost Him Who is all our joy; have not you found Him? Oh, tell us where He is, give Him back to us! My soul is desolate, having lost its treasure. O Joseph, lead us back to Jesus and Mary! O Mary, lead us back to Jesus and Joseph! O Jesus, lead us back to Mary and Joseph and Thyself! Let us again find all three, to praise and bless all three, to love all three with perfect love, in company with the Angels and the Saints, during all eternity! Amen.

* 'Domine, volumus Jesum videre' (Joan. xii. 21).

CHAPTER XII.

ST. JOSEPH is the patron of all Christians,
in all necessities and dangers of life. Now
that the glorious reformer of Carmel and
the great Bishop of Geneva have written so
admirably on the power of the holy spouse
of Mary, who can venture to call this truth
in question? I do not remember, says the
seraphic Teresa of Jesus, to have ever
demanded from this great Saint a single
grace, whether for body or for soul, which
was not granted. This makes me believe
that while God gives to other Saints the
power of helping us in certain special necessities, to St. Joseph He gives the privilege of
helping us in all circumstances where his
protection is needful for us. This is also
taught by St. Francis of Sales, who thus ex-

126

presses himself : ' St. Joseph is in heaven, body and soul ; of that there can be no doubt. Oh! how happy shall we be if we can merit to have part in his holy intercessions! for nothing can be refused to him, either by Our Lady or by her glorious Son.'* Two such witnesses may suffice for the present. Now, let us examine in detail what persons have a special claim to the protection of our great Patriarch.

In the first place, he is the patron of virgins, since he was the first among men to engage himself by vow to perpetual virginity. Secondly, he is the patron of married people, because he was united to the most holy of women by the bonds of a true and most happy marriage. He pledged to her his faith, and received hers, forming with her but one heart and one soul. Thirdly, he is the patron of the fathers of families, since he was by right, and by fact, the head of the Holy Family. Fourthly, he is the patron of working men, for he gained his bread by the sweat of his brow, handling the saw and the plane, and had as apprentice

* *Entretien XIX. sur les vertus de St. Joseph.*

the Son of God, of Whom the inhabitants of Nazareth said, 'Is He not the carpenter's son?' Fifthly, he is the patron of all charged with the education of youth, because, having himself brought up the Son of the Most High, he has received from God a special grace for the protection of childhood and youth. Sixthly, he is the patron of interior souls, since his whole life was passed in contemplation of the sublime virtues of Mary, and of the humanly divine actions of the Incarnate Word. Seventhly, he is the patron of Religious, because he was an excellent master of poverty, chastity and obedience, a perfect model of common life, a living rule for both active and contemplative life. Eighthly, he is the patron of Priests, having been the first of all men to touch with his hands the Sacred Body of the Saviour of the world, and having offered to the Eternal Father the first drops of the precious Blood which the Incarnate Word shed in the circumcision. He also frequently carried Him in his arms with the most tender feelings of piety, love and reverence. Ninthly, he is the patron of Prelates, because, during long

years, in the most painful and difficult circumstances, he governed, with incredible solicitude
and admirable wisdom, the two most holy persons who ever were upon earth, Jesus and
Mary. Tenthly, he is the patron of all who
are in positions of power and dignity, because
the Church sings of him, 'God hath established him the lord of His house, and the
master of all His possessions.'*

There are still other classes of people who
have a special claim on St. Joseph and stand
in special need of his protection : they are the
sinners, the afflicted, and the dying. Of these
we shall treat in the following chapter.

* *Liturg.*, in festo St. Joseph.

CHAPTER XIII.

ST. JOSEPH, SPECIAL PATRON OF SINNERS, OF THE AFFLICTED, AND OF THE DYING.

To complete my subject, I say, in the first place, that St. Joseph is the patron of repentant sinners; and I would here dwell more at length on this consoling subject, had I not already touched upon it at the end of the eleventh chapter. Still, however, I shall add one or two reasons which explain why St. Joseph feels such tender compassion with sinners. It is evident that the same motive which induces Mary to be their refuge, must equally influence her spouse. Would he ever have been the father of the Saviour, had there been no sinners upon earth? Nor can any man understand so well as he does the great misfortune of the sinner in having lost God. He himself once lost the Child

Jesus during three days, and although it was
in no way his fault, how great was his
anguish ! No father ever suffered such sorrow
as did this foster-father ! Judge from this
with what compassion St. Joseph receives the
sinner who confidently implores his help, and
with what ardour he strives to make peace
between him and Jesus.

In the second place, I say that St. Joseph
is the patron of the afflicted. Our Lady once
revealed to St. Bridget that, as the Child Jesus
began to grow up, people went to look at Him
while He laboured in the workshop of His
father.* Little by little they became familiar

---

* According to an ancient custom, which still pre-
vails among the Arabs and other Eastern nations,
Joseph exercised his trade in another house from that
inhabited by Mary. His workshop, in which Jesus
Christ Himself worked, was a low room, ten or twelve
feet long, and as many broad (Orsini, *Histoire de la
Mère de Dieu*, chap. viii.). The same author quotes, as
a note, the following passage from F. de Géramb :
'This house of Joseph is situated about a hundred
and thirty to a hundred and forty paces from that
of St. Ann ; the place is still called *Joseph's workshop*.
A large church was built there, but the Turks have
destroyed part of it. There still remains a chapel,
in which the holy sacrifice of the Mass is daily offered.'
(*Pélerinage à Jérusalem*, par le R. P. de Géramb).
These details are confirmed by' Monseigneur Mislin
(*Les Saints Lieux*, chap. **xxxvi.**).

with Him, and ventured to ask Him questions, to which He replied with rare wisdom. His words were so sweet, and His beauty so attractive, that He inflamed all hearts, and those who were in affliction said : ' Let us go to the Son of Mary, and He will console us ; for this Holy Child seems to be the Master of hearts, moving their springs as He will.' They added : ' See how the Son of Joseph teaches the masters themselves, for a great spirit speaks in Him.'* Many believed He had learned all this from him whom they regarded as His father ; so that the house of Joseph was the refuge of the unfortunate, and the consolation of the afflicted. Those were esteemed happy who, possessing the friendship of this holy man, could, through him, obtain the privilege of speaking with the Divine Child, Who was the Wisdom of the world. We, too, would find ourselves effectually relieved in all our troubles, were we to say to ourselves : ' Let us go to Joseph, and to the Son of Joseph ; let

---

* ' Cujus visus et locutio sic mirabilis erat, ut multi tribulati dicerent : Eamus ad Filium Mariæ, a quo possumus consolari. Ecce Filius Joseph docet magistros ; aliquis spiritus magnus loquitur in eo ' (S. Brigitt., *Revelat.,* lib. vi, c. 58).

us not leave them till our hearts are filled with
heavenly consolation, for with them is Paradise,'
And this can be done quite as well now as then;
Jesus Christ is still as kind as He then was,
and as willing to help us. But in order to
approach Him with true confidence, let us
first turn to His foster-father, let us ask him
to intercede on our behalf: He that chose to
be subject to him on earth, can refuse him
nothing in heaven.

In the third place, St. Joseph is the patron
of the dying. If it be so important during life-
time, on the stormy sea of the world, to have
a powerful protector, how much more is it so
at the supreme and decisive moment on which
eternity depends! For the just man, a holy
death is the crown of good works and of
all virtues; for the repentant sinner, it is
the renunciation, the solemn reparation of all
past faults; for both, it is the end of all
evil, and the beginning of unending bliss.
But among all the Saints of God, to whom
shall we address ourselves in preference, to
obtain for us this most precious of all
blessings. We cannot hesitate. Joseph is
the father of our Judge; he will gain our

pardon. His power is terrible to the enemies of our salvation ; he will put them to flight. Never was there a death so sweet and so privileged as that of Joseph; he will obtain for us also the grace of a sweet and holy death.

I do not, then, fear to speak incorrectly, nor to displease the august Queen of Heaven, in applying to her holy spouse the words spoken by St. Bernard about herself : ' He offers to all men the help of his protection. By invoking him, the just man receives grace ; the sinner, pardon ; the afflicted, consolation ; the sick, recovery, or patience in suffering ; the dying, sweet confidence in the merits of the Saviour ; in a word, all receive of his fulness, and are loaded with his benefits.'*

* *Serm. in Signum magnum*, n. 2.

CHAPTER XIV.

ON DIFFERENT DEVOTIONS WHICH MAY BE PRACTISED IN HONOUR OF THE GLORIOUS ST. JOSEPH.

WE do not praise the Saints merely for the sake of praising them; as St. Bernard says, they are so full of heaven's gifts that our poor praises can scarcely add anything to their glory. We praise them in order to admire them; we admire them in order to love them; we love them in order to serve them; we serve them in order to imitate them; and by imitating them we gain their favour, and merit to have them as protectors in heaven. It is glorious for St. Joseph to be so great, but what do we gain by his greatness if he do not share it with us, if he be not our advocate on high? Now he is willing to be of service to us if we show ourselves worthy, if we render him some poor service, and offer him really heart-felt homage. It is certainly praiseworthy to recite prayers in his honour, to adorn his statue with flowers, or even to receive Holy Communion on the day of his feast. All that is good, but there are other pious practices which we may add ; and I shall mention some which are well suited to aid those whose sweet ambition it is to gain the love and favour of the glorious Patriarch, whose power is so great in heaven.

First Devotion.—The best devotion to St. Joseph is to imitate his virtues, to model your actions on his, and to act as he acted. He and Our Lady will accept your feeble efforts and help you, and God will give you His blessing.

Second Devotion.—Say attentively every day some short prayer in honour of St. Joseph, and if your devotion inclines you to it, apply to him some of the invocations addressed to Our Lady in her litanies ; with the exception of a few which belong exclusively to the Mother of God, they require but little alteration to be appropriate to St. Joseph. Try this practice, and your heart will derive from it both contentment and profit.

Third Devotion.—From time to time consecrate an entire week to the glorious St. Joseph, that he may offer all you do to Mary, to Jesus, to the Most Holy Trinity, and that he may dispose, acccording to his pleasure, of the fruit of your good works.

Fourth Devotion.—Choose seven titles of honour, one for each day of the week, by which to do homage to this great Saint, and vary your devotion. The first day you may honour him as spouse of Our Lady; the second, as father of the Saviour; the third, as model of virginity and chastity; the fourth, as the most faithful and most favoured of patriarchs; the fifth, as governor of Jesus and Mary; the sixth, as fosterer of the Holy Family; the seventh, as guardian of the Infant Jesus, and distributer of the treasures of the Messias.

Fifth Devotion.—For the feast of St. Joseph, do not be satisfied with one day, which is not enough for the honour of so great and holy a patron, but celebrate the entire octave. Each day of the octave either say or hear Mass, communicate in his honour, or give alms according to your means; better still, if you can, do all that at once; he will render it to you a hundredfold in heaven. Has he not often come at the hour of death to console his devout servants? Has he not shown himself to them in the company of his holy spouse, and of her and his Son, Jesus Christ? Were he to do the same for you, you would deem yourself amply rewarded for your devotion to him.

Sixth Devotion.—Imitate those who, every Wednesday, in honour of St. Joseph, either say Mass, or cause a Mass to be said, which they attend. If you wish to do still more, make a perpetual foundation, so that, till the end of the world, God may be glorified by your means.

Seventh Devotion.—Try to win others to the devotion to St. Joseph; speak often of him, and more from the heart than only from the lips; words strike but the ear, while eloquence from the heart gains other hearts. A celebrated preacher was wonderfully consoled at the hour of his death, when Our Lady appeared to him and told him she came to assist him, because of his holy practice of relating, in each of his sermons, some story in her honour, or in that of her chaste spouse. The same glorious Virgin deigned to thank St. Teresa for having reawakened devotion to St. Joseph throughout the Church.

Eighth Devotion.—Always have in your oratory, or upon your heart, the picture of this great and amiable Saint. Lay all your troubles at his feet; speak to him familiarly as if he were present; in all your necessities go to him; in life and death take him for your advocate. Should you lose every other support, remember, and believe with certainty, that Jesus, Mary, and Joseph will never fail you.

Ninth Devotion.—When you receive Holy Communion, unite yourself spiritually to Our Lady and St. Joseph, and, with them, keep the Child Jesus company, as they did when they carried Him to the temple to present Him to His Father. Your heart is then the true temple of the Lord. Say to Him lovingly that to-day the feast of the Presentation is celebrated in your soul; and should Mary and Joseph desire to ransom the Divine Child, tell them that He has been given to you by God the Father, that they themselves are the two

doves whom you demand for the ransom of
Jesus, and that you will be contented with
none else.

Tenth Devotion.—'Never,' says Gerson, 'did
anyone worship St. Joseph with more honour
and veneration than the holy Virgin. She
considered him as her lord, as her spouse, as
the foster-father of Jesus, as the man the
most holy on earth, as the master who had
been given to her by God Himself. In sick-
ness and in health, she served him with the
greatest tenderness.' The Chancellor of Paris,
in the poem called 'Josephina,' which he composed in honour of St. Joseph, describes with
singular pleasure, in verses of charming simplicity, the assiduous care which Our Lady
unceasingly lavished on him from whom she
herself had received so many services. Imitate her as far as you can, and beg her to
teach you true devotion to her holy spouse.

Eleventh Devotion.—Make an irrevocable
contract in presence of the Celestial Court,
and under the eyes of the august and adorable Trinity. Give to Mary and to Joseph your
body, your soul, your heart, your entire self;
and then say, with St. Catherine of Siena:

'Now I recommend to you your heart, and your poor servant. I no longer belong to myself, but to both of you. I ask but one thing of you : keep what belongs to you ; never permit me to take it back from your blessed hands. This is my irrevocable resolution, for all eternity to belong entirely to Jesus, to Mary, and to Joseph, and I renounce, as far as it is possible for me to do so, all power of ever revoking this promise.'

Twelfth Devotion.—The gift of yourself is unquestionably more desirable and agreeable to Mary and Joseph than aught else; yet if God has granted you means, dedicate to them a more or less considerable share of what you possess. A great Saint, who, after having been patrician and consul, shed his blood for Jesus Christ, employed his immense riches in solacing the sick and the poor, serving them with his own hands.* Now, while the memory of Roman emperors is held in affection by no one, the name of this holy man is not forgotten, and his memory is held in benediction on earth, and still more in heaven. Do you similar acts of charity in honour of St. Joseph.

* St. Gallican, *Roman Martyrology*, 25th June.

Thirteenth Devotion. — There have been noble and wealthy persons who have erected churches or chapels in honour of the spouse of Mary, with a privileged altar for the solace of the souls in purgatory.

Fourteenth Devotion.—Undertake the maintenance of a young scholar, in the hope that he may one day become a good Priest, or holy Religious ; or help a poor girl in honour of St. Joseph. This devotion is most pleasing to him, for its effects are real, and its results solid and lasting.*

---

* This kind of devotion deserves to be illustrated by some examples. The maire of a village in France, to whom God had not granted children, proposed to his wife that they should bring up two orphan boys in their house. After a time he placed them first in a college, and later in the diocesan seminary, and both became Priests. A lady, whose fortune was not large, nevertheless managed constantly to maintain either a student in the seminary, or a young Religious in the novitiate of missionaries. In a country not far from France, a man of high rank, but whose fortune neither equalled his position nor the generosity of his disposition, had saved a sum of 600 francs for a journey of recreation. On the point of setting out he heard that a young girl was in danger of losing her innocence and her soul, if she could not procure a dowry of at least 600 francs. The dowry was at once paid, and the proposed excursion given up.—*Note of the Editor.*

Fifteenth Devotion.—The Chancellor of
Paris was very devout and very ingenious
in his devotion. In his old age he was most
assiduous in teaching the children of Lyons
the Catechism, and at the end of each lesson
he made those little innocents pray, ' My God,
my Creator, be merciful to your poor servant
John Gerson !' Their voices brought tears to
the eyes of all who heard them, and drew
down the mercies of God upon this virtuous
man, who died a holy death Do you then,
in a similar manner, unite your heart with
all those hearts who love St. Joseph ; unite
your voice and your affections with those
of all the Saints in Paradise, of all the just
upon earth, of all the holy souls in purgatory, and say to God, to Our Lady, and
to St. Joseph, that you approve of all that
others do and say in their honour ; that were
it in your power to do as much as they together do, you would assuredly do it with
all your heart, and with all your strength.
Thank all the Saints for the homage they pay
to this great Patriarch, entreat them to re-
double their praises, as far as the laws of
heaven and the decrees of Divine Providence

permit them. As you cannot take part in their canticles, beg at least to be their echo, and tell them you ratify whatever they do and have done in honour of St. Joseph.

Sixteenth Devotion.—The last devotion which I propose to you is the avowal of your own insufficiency. It seems to me that St. Joseph, contemplating the Incarnate Word in the lowly house of Nazareth, must often have said in his heart: 'I adhere to all that my spouse says; I unite myself with all that she does; I take part in all her desires. I do not speak myself: but I hope that, as I agree with all that she thinks well to say, Jesus will approve of my silence. She and I are one in heart; she says all; I say nothing except through her mouth and her heart.' Reader, do the same; repeat to Our Lady that you approve and ratify all she says and does in honour of her spouse, and that you thank her for all a thousand times. Add that it is not the want of cordial affection which makes you silent, but rather its excess, because you can find no words to express it, and your tongue cannot keep pace with your feelings. Say that since St. Joseph by his silence

has said as much as, and more than all others,
you desire to imitate him.

St. John tells us that when the Lamb had
opened the seventh seal of the mysterious
book mentioned in the Apocalypse, there was
silence in heaven, as it were, for half an hour;
all the Saints were as if entranced, and could
do nothing but admire the infinite majesty
of God. So may you also do. Tell St.
Joseph that while others do wonderful things,
your part must be to humble yourself, and
acknowledge your own nothingness; while
they offer their love, you can but offer nothingness and abjection, and acknowledge
yourself incapable and unworthy of speaking.
Fear not to imitate St. Augustine and other
Saints who complained of God to God Himself, in some such terms as these: ' Thou com-
mandest me to love Thee, O God most worthy
of love; why, then, hast Thou given me such
a poor and narrow heart ? Why art Thou so
great and I so little ? The object being infinite, should not the heart and love be infinite
also ?' Then you may continue: ' Thou hast
made St. Joseph so great; Thou inspirest me
with the ardent desire to love him, and yet

Thou seest how incapable I am of doing anything worthy of Thee or of him. Assist my weakness, I beseech Thee, O Lord! I desire to do what is right, but I have not the power. Give me the power to do more. At any rate, be satisfied to see one who desires more than he is able to perform, who would fain do all that can be done by all men and all Saints, so as to honour Thee in the great things Thou hast done to St. Joseph.

And now, reader, I have come to the end of what I had to say to you about the glorious St. Joseph. Pardon me if I have expressed myself in terms which may obscure rather than explain the glory of this great Patriarch, excuse me if I have rather cooled than inflamed your devotion. I am certain of the indulgence of the holy spouse of Mary, who sees in my heart the most sincere desire to please him; and so I hope for your indulgence also, unless, indeed, you be less desirous to imitate his kindness than his other virtues.

St. Joseph our Helper in Every Variety of Necessity.

1. VENERATE ST. JOSEPH IF YOU WISH TO DIE HAPPILY.

A VENETIAN merchant had the habit of daily visiting an image of St. Joseph which stood in a niche at the corner of one of the streets of the town in which he lived.

Falling sick of a dangerous illness, which soon brought him to the brink of the grave, St. Joseph appeared to him as his last moments approached. At the sight of the Saint, towards whom he had ever been so devout, the sick man was filled with consolation, but above all his conscience became so enlightened, that in an instant he seemed to perceive clearly all the sins of his past life, and in their full heinousness and guilt; while at the same time he felt a new and exceeding great contrition, together with the sweetest hope of pardon.

As a priest was present with him, he made a fresh and fervent confession, and having received absolution, full of peace and joy, piously expired in our Lord.

2. MARY AND JOSEPH.

The venerable servant of God, Alexis of Vigevano, a Capuchin, ended his meritorious life with a death full of sweetness.

A few moments before his departure he asked one of the brothers to light some candles. They were astonished at his request, and wanted to know the reason of it.

'Our dear Ladye is coming presently with her Spouse, and therefore it is fitting to light candles, that they may both be received with the greatest reverence.'

Soon they perceived that the visit he had predicted had already come to pass, for the dying Father exclaimed, radiant with joy:

'There comes the Queen of Heaven! There comes St. Joseph! Kneel down, my brethren, to receive them reverently.'

But he was now to reap the fruits of this

heavenly visitation, for at the same moment, in the presence of Mary and Joseph, he breathed out his soul into their hands.

It was the 19th of March, the day of triumph for St. Joseph, who visited this good religious on his feast day, to reward him for the loving devotion he had always shown to him.

3. St. Joseph, Teacher of Prayer.

Prayer and meditation are the food of interior life. Therefore we should beseech St. Joseph that he may obtain for us the grace to be very faithful in these two practices, and that we may perform them in a right manner.

Saint Teresa says :

' Let him who needs a guide to lead him on in the way of prayer and meditation take St. Joseph as a master, for he will show him the right path, and safely conduct him to a good termination.'

Father Barry relates:

' A religious desired once, as she herself confessed to me, to be freed from her distractions in prayer. In order to obtain this grace, she felt herself inspired to have recourse to St.

Joseph. She did so with great devotion, and the gift of prayer was bestowed on her in a high measure.'

4. FATHER PICOT DE CLORIVIÈRE.

This saintly priest was a member of the congregation of the Sacred Heart in the time of the terrible French Revolution. It seems that he had obtained from St. Joseph the grace of an ever-increasing love to the most Holy Sacrament of the Altar. Against all expectation, he was ordained priest; but he had so great an impediment in his speech, that he would have been unable to give himself to the apostolic labours if he had not been cured of this defect in a miraculous manner. Then he preached in many churches, and as his only reward, he desired to obtain through the intercession of St. Joseph from God the grace to die at the foot of the Altar in adoration of the most Holy Sacrament, without being a burden to anyone. St. Joseph who is so powerful over the Heart of Jesus, certainly pleaded for the request of his client. For one Sunday, when, as usual, Father Picot de Clorivière went to the chapel in order to pay a

visit to Our Lord in the Blessed Sacrament.
He knelt down, and as his weakness did not
allow of his kneeling upright without support,
he leant his elbow on a railing which separated
the sanctuary from the church. Then he
began to pray ; but his soul followed his
prayer, and ascended also on high before the
Throne of God. One of the Fathers, who had
just before heard his confession and given him
absolution, was witness of this holy death.
He died at the age of eighty-five years.

5. St. Joseph a Guide on the Road.

A pious lay-brother of the great Benedictine
monastery of Monserrat in Spain, had the
custom of venerating with particular devotion
the mystery of the Flight into Egypt.

His heart especially grieved at all St. Joseph
had to suffer, when he had to fly in such great
poverty and haste, with Jesus and Mary, into
a strange and idolatrous country. It once
happened that this brother had to return to
his monastery from a great distance. Already
the shadows of evening were falling, it began
to grow dark, and the monastery was still far
off. Suddenly he perceived that he had lost

his way, and he feared that he should have to
spend the night in the open air, surrounded by
dangerous precipices ; and it was the more sad
as, to the dangers of the mountains, was added
the fear of the wild beasts, which he knew
infested those parts.

All of a sudden, whilst he was full of those
anxious thoughts, he saw not far off a man,
who led a donkey by a bridle. Seated on its
back was a lady of exceedingly great beauty,
with a most noble and majestic appearance.
In her arms rested a little sleeping child.
The Brother hastened forward to meet the
stranger in order to ask him to direct him in
the right way. But his joy at this sight
increased still more, and was mixed with sweet
consolation, as the unknown man bade him
follow him, and promised to guide him to the
monastery.

Whilst they pursued their way, conversations of wonderful unction refreshed the heart
of the Brother ; but scarcely was the monastery
gate in view, than suddenly the guide and his
family disappeared from before his eyes, and
nowhere was the least trace of them to be
discovered. But in the heart of the Brother
awoke the joyful conviction that St. Joseph

himself had been his guide, and that he had rewarded in this manner his devotion to his sorrow, in the mystery of the Flight into Egypt.

6. A Beautiful Death of a Faithful Client of St. Joseph.

The venerable Franciscan Nun, Prudentia Zagnoni, who was renowned for her extraordinary virtues, had during her whole life a most fervent devotion to St. Joseph. In return, at her death she received an exceeding great favour; for the Saint appeared to her and assisted her in her agony. In order to give her still more consolation, he held in his arms Him Who is the joy of the Angels, the Divine Child Jesus.

The good nun drew from this sight the sweetest consolation and delight; her joy was not to be described, and the nuns who were present assisting at her agony were much touched as they heard her conversing now with St. Joseph and now with the Divine Child, thanking them for their visit, and declaring that she already tasted beforehand the joys of Paradise.

From her looks and gestures, it was evident to all around that St. Joseph had given her the Divine Child to caress in her arms, thus giving to his faithful servant the highest proof of his favour that he was able in the moment of her greatest need and extremity.

7. St. Joseph a Master of the Interior Life.

A Father of the Society of Jesus, being on a journey, met one day a young man with whom he entered into conversation. He very soon recognised in him a chosen soul, rich in graces and rare gifts, so that he could not remember ever to have found a soul more advanced in perfection.

But his astonishment increased as he learned that no one had ever instructed the young man concerning the lessons of a spiritual life; yet he heard him speaking on the most sublime subjects like a saint and a theologian. As the Father could not understand how this could be, he asked the young man where he had gained this wisdom and spiritual knowledge.

' Ten years ago,' he replied, ' God inspired me

to choose St. Joseph for my patron saint and guide; all that I have learnt has been from him.'

Then he spoke of the sanctity of the Foster-Father of Jesus, and concluded his conversation with the assurance that this Saint was the special guide and protector of those souls, who led a hidden and interior life.

8. How St. Joseph rewards those who Promote his Honour.

When Father Lallemant was Rector of the Jesuit College at Bourges, he called two of the young professors and promised each of them that they should receive that grace which they most desired, if they would exhort their scholars to venerate St. Joseph, and offer him some particular homage on his feast, which was just then approaching. The two professors joyfully agreed to this proposal, and they so zealously encouraged their scholars that on the feast of St. Joseph both classes received Holy Communion in his honour, besides performing other practices of devotion.

On the same day, the two professors went to the Father-Rector, and revealed to him secretly the particular grace which they were each desirous to receive. The first was the celebrated Fr. Nouet, who desired the grace to be able to write and to speak worthily of our Divine Saviour. It is not known what grace the second asked for, but it is known for certain that he, as well as Fr. Nouet, obtained what he desired.

APPENDIX.

A Notice on the Cord of St. Joseph.

I.—Its Origin.

THE devotion to the Cord of St. Joseph took its rise in the town of Antwerp (Belgium), in the year 1657, in consequence of a miraculous cure effected by the wearing of this precious girdle.

At the above epoch there lived at Antwerp an Augustinian nun remarkable for her piety, called Sister Elizabeth, who, during three years, had suffered excruciating pains, occasioned by a most cruel distemper. She had then reached such a stage that the physicians, seeing no resource possible, declared her death to be inevitable, and fast approaching. Losing all hope in human aid, the Sister addressed herself to Heaven, and having always had a particular devotion to St. Joseph, she prayed him to intercede with our Lord for her recovery. At the same time she had a cord blessed in the Saint's honour, girded herself with it, and a few days after, as she was praying before his image, she found herself all of a sudden freed from pain. Those who knew the disease and its nature, in her instance, declared her recovery miraculous. An authentic act was drawn up in presence of a public notary, and a Protestant physician could not help proclaiming the truth.

This fact, related by the Bollandists, was admitted by the author of a 'Month of St. Joseph,' published at Rome in 1810. The reading of this book in 1842, in St. Nicholas's Church at Verona, where the devotion of the Month of March was beginning to be practised, brought to the knowledge of several persons the event above related. Immediately, in imitation of the religious of Antwerp, many patients, animated by a tender piety towards St. Joseph, procured a cord blessed in the Church of St. Nicholas, where there is a chapel (since become a celebrated sanctuary) consecrated to the Saint.

Numerous special graces were obtained, and

the devotion soon spread rapidly. Hundreds of cords were despatched to France, Belgium, all parts of Italy, and even to America and Asia.

The Cord of St. Joseph was asked, not merely as a remedy against bodily ailments, but also as a preservative of the virtue of purity. Ere long, his lordship the Bishop of Verona became aware of the necessity of addressing a supplication to the Congregation of Rites, which he did by a letter bearing date January 14, 1859. After a mature examination the Sacred Congregation, in accordance with the request, approved, by a Rescript of September 19, 1859, the new formula of blessing, and permitted its solemn and private use. Finally, his lordship obtained for the Association of the Cord of St. Joseph the privilege of being declared 'primarie,' and at the same time His Holiness Pope Pius IX. enriched it with precious indulgences.

II.—Graces Attached to the Wearing of the Cord of St. Joseph.

Graces precious to the piety of St. Joseph's servants are attached to the wearing of his cord. They are:—1st, St. Joseph's special protection; 2, purity of soul; 3, the grace of chastity; 4, final perseverance; 5, particular assistance at the hour of death.

III.—NATURE OF THE CORD AND MANNER OF WEARING IT.

The Cord of St. Joseph should be of thread or cotton, ending at one extremity in seven knots, indicative of the joyful, dolorous, and glorious mysteries of the august Patriarch.

It is worn as a girdle, and ought to be blessed by a priest possessing powers to engird one with it.

IV.—PRAYERS OF THE HOLY CORD.

Recite daily in honour of St. Joseph seven times Gloria Patri, together with the following prayer:

O St. Joseph, Father and Protector of Virgins, to whose faithful custody Christ Jesus, Innocence itself, and Mary Virgin of Virgins, were committed; I pray and beseech thee by these dear pledges Jesus and Mary, that being preserved from all uncleanness, I may with spotless mind, pure heart and chaste body, ever most chastely serve Jesus and Mary all the days of my life. Amen.

V. Plenary Indulgences attached to the Cord of St. Joseph.

1. On the day of entrance into the Association.

2. On the day of the Feast of the Espousals of the Blessed Virgin and St. Joseph (January 23rd).

3. On the 19th of March, the Feast of St. Joseph, and on one of the seven days which immediately follow that festival.

4. On the Patronage of St. Joseph (3rd Sunday after Easter).

5. At the article of death, for all the Associates who, being truly penitent, and having confessed their sins, shall receive the Holy Viaticum ; or who, not being able to do this, shall invoke with the mouth or at least with the heart the Name of Jesus.

Conditions for gaining the said Indulgences.

1. To be truly contrite, and to confess and communicate.

2. To visit the church or chapel of the Association or any other church or public oratory.

3. To pray there for peace between Christian princes, the extirpation of heresies, and the exaltation of our holy Mother the Church.

The plenary indulgence of a privileged altar is attached to all Masses celebrated for a departed Associate.

An indulgence of seven years and seven quarantines on each of the Sundays which come immediately after the Ember Saturdays for the Associates who shall visit with a contrite heart the church of the Arch-Confraternity, and there pray for the intentions of the Sovereign Pontiff.

All these indulgences are applicable to the souls in Purgatory.

FINIS.

PRAYERS TO ST. JOSEPH

THE LITANY OF ST. JOSEPH

Lord, have mercy on us.
Christ, have mercy on us.

Lord, have mercy on us. Christ, hear us.
Christ, graciously hear us.

God the Father of Heaven, *have mercy on us.*
God the Son, Redeemer of the world,
God the Holy Ghost,
Holy Trinity, One God,

Holy Mary, *pray for us.*
St. Joseph,
Renowned offspring of David,
Light of Patriarchs,
Spouse of the Mother of God,
Chaste guardian of the Virgin,
Foster father of the Son of God,

Diligent protector of Christ,
Head of the Holy Family,
Joseph most just,
Joseph most chaste,
Joseph most prudent,
Joseph most strong,
Joseph most obedient,
Joseph most faithful,
Mirror of patience,
Lover of poverty,
Model of artisans,
Glory of home life,
Guardian of virgins,
Pillar of families,
Solace of the afflicted,
Hope of the sick,
Patron of the dying,
Terror of demons,
Protector of Holy Church,

Lamb of God, Who takest away
the sins of the world,
Spare us, O Lord!

Lamb of God, Who takest away
the sins of the world,
Graciously hear us, O Lord!

Lamb of God, Who takest away
the sins of the world,
Have mercy on us.

V. He made him the lord of His household.
R. *And prince over all His possessions.*

Let us pray.

O GOD, Who in Thy ineffable Providence
didst vouchsafe to choose Blessed Joseph
to be the spouse of Thy most holy Mother,
grant, we beseech Thee, that we may have for
our advocate in Heaven him whom we venerate
as our protector on earth. Who livest and
reignest world without end. Amen.

NOVENA TO ST. JOSEPH

O GLORIOUS St. Joseph, faithful follower of
Jesus Christ, to thee do we raise our
hearts and hands, to implore thy powerful intercession in obtaining from the benign Heart of
Jesus all the helps and graces necessary for our
spiritual and temporal welfare, particularly the
grace of a happy death, and the special favor we
now implore *(mention your petition).*

(Then say the following seven times in honor of the seven sorrows and joys of St. Joseph.)

O Glorious St. Joseph! Through the love thou bearest to Jesus Christ and for the glory of His Name, hear our prayers and obtain our petitions. Jesus, Mary and Joseph, assist us.

MEMORARE OF ST. JOSEPH

REMEMBER, O most illustrious Patriarch St. Joseph, on the testimony of St. Teresa, thy devoted client, never has it been heard that anyone invoked thy protection or sought thy mediation who has not obtained relief. In this confidence I come before thee, my loving protector, chaste Spouse of Mary, foster-father of the Saviour of men and dispenser of the treasures of His Sacred Heart. Despise not my earnest prayer but graciously hear and obtain my petition.

Let us pray.

O God, Who by Thy ineffable Providence didst vouchsafe to choose Blessed Joseph for the spouse of Thy most holy Mother, grant, we beseech Thee, that he whom we venerate as our protector on earth may be our intercessor in Heaven. Who livest and reignest for ever and ever. Amen.

PRAYER FOR A HAPPY DEATH

O GLORIOUS St. Joseph, behold I choose thee today for my special patron in life and at the hour of my death. Preserve and increase in me the spirit of prayer and fervor in the service of God. Remove far from me every kind of sin; obtain for me that my death may not come upon me unawares, but that I may have time to confess my sins sacramentally, and to bewail them with a most perfect understanding and a most sincere contrition, in order that I may breathe forth my soul into the hands of Jesus and Mary. Amen.

PRAYER FOR SUCCESS IN WORK

GLORIOUS St. Joseph, model of all those who are devoted to labor, obtain for me the grace to work conscientiously, putting the call of duty above my natural inclinations; to work with gratitude and joy, considering it an honor to employ and develop, by means of labor, the gifts received from God, without recoiling before weariness or difficulties; to work, above all, with purity of intention, and with detachment from self, having always death before my eyes and the account which I must render of time lost, of talents wasted, of good omitted, of vain complacency in success, so fatal to the work of God. All for Jesus, all for Mary, all after thy example, O Patriarch St. Joseph. Such shall be my watchword in life and death.

PRAYER FOR PURITY

SAINT Joseph, father and guardian of virgins, into whose faithful keeping were entrusted Innocency itself, Christ Jesus, and Mary, the Virgin of virgins, I pray and beseech thee, through Jesus and Mary, those pledges so dear to thee, to keep me from all uncleanness, and to grant that my mind may be untainted, my heart pure and my body chaste; help me always to serve Jesus and Mary in perfect chastity. Amen.

PRAYER TO OBTAIN A SPECIAL FAVOR

O BLESSED Saint Joseph, tenderhearted father, faithful guardian of Jesus, chaste spouse of the Mother of God, we pray and beseech thee to offer to God the Father, His divine Son, bathed in blood on the cross for sinners, and through the thrice-holy Name of Jesus, obtain for us from the eternal Father the favor we implore.

Appease the Divine anger so justly inflamed by our crimes, beg of Jesus mercy for thy children. Amid the splendors of eternity, forget not the sorrows of those who suffer, those who pray, those who weep; stay the Almighty arm which smites us, that by thy prayers and those of thy most holy Spouse, the Heart of Jesus may be moved to pity and to pardon. Amen.

Saint Joseph, Pray For Us.

THIRTY DAYS' PRAYER TO ST. JOSEPH
For Any Special Intention

EVER BLESSED and glorious Joseph, kind and loving father, and helpful friend of all in sorrow! Thou art the good father and protector of orphans, the defender of the defenseless, the patron of those in need and sorrow. Look kindly on my request. My sins have drawn down on me the just displeasure of my God, and so I am surrounded with unhappiness. To thee, loving guardian of the Family of Nazareth, do I go for help and protection.

Listen, then, I beg of thee, with fatherly concern to my earnest prayers and obtain for me the favor I ask.

I ask it by the infinite mercy of the eternal Son of God, which moved Him to take our nature and to be born into this world of sorrow.

I ask it by the weariness and suffering thou didst endure when thou didst find no shelter at the inn of Bethlehem for the holy Virgin, nor a place where the Son of God could be born. Then, being everywhere refused, thou hadst to allow the Queen of Heaven to give birth to the world's Redeemer in a cave.

I ask it by the loveliness and power of that sacred Name, Jesus, which thou didst confer on the adorable Infant.

I ask it by that painful torture thou didst feel at the prophecy of holy Simeon, which declared the Child Jesus and His holy Mother future victims of our sins and of their great love for us.

I ask it through thy sorrow and pain of soul when the angel declared to thee that the life of the Child Jesus was sought by His enemies. From their evil plan thou hadst to flee with Him and His Blessed Mother into Egypt. I ask it by all the suffering, weariness, and labors of that long and dangerous journey.

I ask it by all thy care to protect the Sacred Child and His Immaculate Mother during thy second journey, when thou wast ordered to return to thy own country. I ask it by thy peaceful life in Nazareth where thou didst meet with so many joys and sorrows.

I ask it by thy great distress when the adorable Child was lost to thee and His Mother for three days. I ask it by thy joy at finding Him in the Temple, and by the comfort thou didst find at Nazareth, while living in the company of the Child Jesus. I ask it by the wonderful submission He showed in His obedience to thee.

I ask it by the perfect love and conformity thou didst show in accepting the Divine order to depart from this life, and from the company of Jesus and Mary. I ask it by the joy which filled thy soul, when the Redeemer of the world, triumphant over death and Hell, entered into the possession of His kingdom and led thee into it with special honors.

I ask it through Mary's glorious Assumption and through that endless happiness thou hast with her in the presence of God.

O good father! I beg of thee, by all thy sufferings, sorrows, and joys, to hear me and obtain for me what I ask. *(Here mention your petitions or think of them.)*

Obtain for all those who have asked my prayers everything that is useful to them in the plan of God. Finally, my dear patron and father, be with me and all who are dear to me in our last moments, that we may eternally sing the praises of

Jesus, Mary and Joseph!

A blameless life, O St. Joseph, may we lead, by thy kind patronage from danger freed. Amen.

A NOVENA PRAYER TO ST. JOSEPH

(To be said four times a day)

O MY GOD, I thank Thee for St. Joseph's devotion to grace.

Lord Jesus, I humbly beseech Thee that I too will be truly devoted to grace.

St. Joseph, if it meets with God's Holy Will, I humbly and urgently ask that my prayer will be granted. *(Mention your petition.)*

O my God, I thank Thee for St. Joseph's devotion to the interior life.

Lord Jesus, I humbly beseech Thee that I too will be truly devoted to the interior life.

St. Joseph, if it meets with God's Holy Will, I humbly and urgently ask that my prayer will be granted. *(Again, mention your petition.)*

O my God, I thank Thee for St. Joseph's devotion to the Divine Child.

Lord Jesus, I humbly beseech Thee that I too will be truly devoted to the Divine Child.

St. Joseph, if it meets with God's Holy Will, I humbly and urgently ask that my prayer will be granted. *(Again, mention your petition.)*

O my God, I thank Thee for St. Joseph's
  devotion to Our Lady.

Lord Jesus, I humbly beseech Thee that I too
  will be truly devoted to Our Lady.

St. Joseph, if it meets with God's Holy Will, I
  humbly and urgently ask that my prayer will
  be granted. *(Again, mention your petition.)*
  Amen.

PRAYER FOR THE
WELFARE OF THE CHURCH

TO THEE, O Blessed Joseph, do we have
recourse in our tribulation, and having im-
plored the help of thy thrice-holy Spouse, we
confidently invoke thy patronage also. By that
charity wherewith thou wast united to the Immaculate Virgin Mother of God, and by that
fatherly affection with which thou didst
embrace the Child Jesus, we beseech thee and
we humbly pray, that thou wouldst look graciously upon the inheritance which Jesus Christ
hath purchased by His Blood, and assist us in
our needs by thy power and strength. Most
watchful guardian of the Holy Family, protect
the chosen people of Jesus Christ; keep far from
us, most loving father, all blight of error and

corruption; mercifully assist us from Heaven, most mighty defender, in this our conflict with the powers of darkness; and, even as of old thou didst rescue the Child Jesus from the supreme peril of His life, so now defend God's holy Church from the snares of the enemy and from all adversity; keep us one and all under thy continual protection, that, supported by thine example and thine assistance, we may be enabled to lead a holy life, die a happy death and come at last to the possession of everlasting blessedness in Heaven. Amen.

PRAYER FOR THE
TRIUMPH OF THE CHURCH

O GLORIOUS Saint Joseph, chosen by God to be the foster-father of Jesus, the chaste spouse of Mary ever Virgin, and the head of the Holy Family, and then appointed by the Vicar of Christ to be the heavenly patron and defender of the Church founded by Jesus, most confidently do I implore at this moment thy powerful aid for all the Church Militant on earth. Do thou shield with thy truly paternal love especially the Supreme Pontiff and all the

Bishops and priests who are in union with the Holy See of Peter. Be the defender of all who labor for souls amidst the trials and tribulations of this life, and cause all the peoples of the earth to submit themselves in a docile spirit to that Church which is the ark of salvation for all men.

Be pleased also, dear Saint Joseph, to accept this dedication of myself which I now make unto thee. I dedicate myself wholly to thee, that thou mayest ever be my father, my patron and my guide in the way of salvation. Obtain for me great purity of heart and a fervent devotion to the interior life. Grant that, following thine example, I may direct all my actions to the greater glory of God, in union with the Sacred Heart of Jesus and the Immaculate Heart of Mary and in union with thee. Finally, pray for me, that I may be a partaker in the peace and joy which were thine at the hour of thy holy death. Amen.